Inside the Minds of
Healthcare Serial Killers

Also By Katherine Ramsland

Inside the Minds of Mass Murderers: Why They Kill

Inside the Minds of Serial Killers: Why They Kill

The Criminal Mind

The Human Predator

Beating the Devil's Game

The Forensic Science of CSI

The CSI Effect

The Science of Cold Case Files

Inside the Minds of Healthcare Serial Killers

Why They Kill

KATHERINE RAMSLAND

Westport, Connecticut
London

Library of Congress Cataloging-in-Publication Data

Ramsland, Katherine M., 1953–
    Inside the minds of healthcare serial killers : why they kill / Katherine
Ramsland.
        p. cm.
    Includes bibliographical references and index.
    ISBN-13: 978–0–275–99422–8 (alk. paper)
    ISBN-10: 0–275–99422–8 (alk. paper)
    1. Serial murderers—Psychology—Case studies.   2. Medical personnel—
Psychology—Case studies.   3. Hospital patients—Crimes against—Case studies.
4. Serial murder investigation—Case studies.   5. Criminal behavior—Case
studies.   6. Criminal psychology—Case studies.   I. Title.
    HV6515.R2525 2007
    364.152'3—dc22   2007016232

British Library Cataloguing in Publication Data is available.

Library of Congress Catalog Card Number: 2007016232
ISBN-13: 978–0–275–99422–8
ISBN-10: 0–275–99422–8

First published in 2007

Praeger Publishers, 88 Post Road West, Westport, CT 06881
An imprint of Greenwood Publishing Group, Inc.
www.praeger.com

Printed in the United States of America

The paper used in this book complies with the
Permanent Paper Standard issued by the National
Information Standards Organization (Z39.48–1984).

10 9 8 7 6 5 4 3 2 1

This book is dedicated to my sister, Donna Johnston,
who's been a sheriff's deputy, an EMT, and a nurse,
so she knows what these investigations are all about.

Contents

Acknowledgments

Many areas of investigation are fairly competitive, and information is often restricted from outsiders, but I've been delighted with how open and eager to pool information the researchers are who examine the phenomenon of healthcare serial murder. Among those I've had the good fortune to meet and discuss the contents of this book are Beatrice Crofts Yorker, Paula Lampe, and Robert Forrest, and they have brought my attention to others who have written about the subject. I'm also grateful to the many meticulous individuals who have published books and articles on specific cases.

Among my frequent associates are forensic nurses, and I'd like to thank Dana DeVito in particular for collaborating on several presentations and an article with me, showing me the ins and outs of healthcare facilities.

Another friend and associate, Zachary Lysek, the Northampton County Coroner, has described his role to me in the Cullen case, assisting me with an understanding of a healthcare serial killer operating right in my own backyard. My sister-in-law, Myra, was also aware of the Ann Arbor hospital investigation, and she offered a few details.

To be fair, the project was actually initiated by my enthusiastic editor at Praeger, Suzanne Staszak-Silva, who spotted its potential in something else I had written, so I thank her. I'm also grateful to Marilyn Bardsley, my editor at the Crime Library, because she gave me the initial opportunities to explore the phenomenon.

And, as always, I am deeply indebted to my literary agent, John Silbersack, of Trident Media Group, who always guides me in the right directions—the most interesting ones.

Introduction

Killers in the medical profession seem especially heinous to us because while they have taken a solemn oath to do everything in their power to do no harm, they nevertheless view their patients as guinea pigs. Their motive for becoming healthcare practitioners seems to have more to do with power, control, attention, and personal gain than healing. Victims are readily available and it's not that difficult to cover up certain types of murders in a major hospital, especially if the patients are elderly, very young, or suffer from serious illnesses or injuries.

With the arrest and conviction of a number of healthcare employees since the 1970s who murdered patients in their care, it has become clear to criminologists and psychologists that these offenders occupy a special subcategory among serial killers. While most of them initially claimed they killed from motives of mercy, with *very* few exceptions it turned out that they clearly had other motives, mostly self-centered. The idea that a person might enter an industry committed to caring for others and then exploit the atmosphere of trust to entertain, enrich, or empower themselves is appalling. More than that, it's a wake-up call to an industry entrusted with assisting people while they're in life's most vulnerable conditions.

Not all healthcare professionals who commit murder are serial killers, but we'll make the distinction clear in this book, and then focus primarily on those who kill patients in ways and for reasons that encourage them to repeat their actions. Healthcare serial killers (HCSKs) may be any type of employees in the healthcare system who use their position to murder at least two patients in two separate incidents, with the psychological capacity for more killing. (HCSKs generally do kill more than two people. Because the murders are hard to detect, the HCSK's spate of murders often goes unnoticed longer than, say, those of compulsive lust killers.)

A HCSK might be a physician, nurse, or any of the key support staff, and while some of the predators discussed in the following chapters were convicted of only one murder, they were typically suspected in many more. A number of these cases resulted in acquittal, and while I generally avoid referring to them, an occasional case proved useful to make a point.

In the past three decades, there have been over 85 such cases in civilized societies (half in the United States), with more suspected and several that cannot be fully investigated. A study published in the *Journal of Forensic Science* in November 2006, undertaken by the leading researchers on this phenomenon, examined 90 cases from 20 countries of criminal prosecution of HCSKs that occurred between 1970 and 2006. Fifty-four of the defendants had been convicted, while 24 more were waiting prosecution or the outcome of their trial had not been published. Most of them had used the injection of lethal substances, suffocation, poisoning, and/or equipment tampering to achieve their goals. Of the cases examined, nurses comprised 86 percent, and the number of suspicious deaths among the 54 convicted HCSKs was a shocking 2113.[1]

A few HCSKs enter the profession as predatory angels of death, alert to the opportunities for murder in a clinic or hospital, where the administration of medication is easy and some deaths are already expected; however, many transform into killers on the job. After killing once, usually out of pity, they learn that they enjoy it and so they continue. Understandably, coworkers, hospital administrators, and potential patients want to know how to spot and stop dangerous nurses. That's what this book is about. With the method of case analysis, which includes motives, backgrounds, and the modus operandi of different types of HCSKs, a better understanding of how and why they operate is available.

From intensive study, we now know that within the medical context, serial killers tend to show the same types of behaviors, from one to another, even if driven by different motives. Thus, we can collect a list of red flags that will assist their colleagues and supervisors to recognize the behavioral and personality signals. It's not easy for anyone to accept that a coworker might actually be a killer, and it's hard to be a whistle-blower based on suspicion alone. Yet those who are prepared and who understand the need for documentation and evidence, will realize that the phenomenon of HCSK does occur; that HCSKs are not always convicted; and that the healthcare system does provide conditions that facilitate their deadly deeds. With better awareness, the conviction rate can be improved and the facilitating conditions corrected.

One survey of cases since 1970 shows that the incidents appear to be increasing, with 10 during the 1970s, 21 the following decade, 2 more than that in the 1990s, and 40 in the first half of the present decade.[2] In fact, experts speculate that healthcare has contributed more serial killers than all other professions combined.[3]

Let's look at the details of a recent case, so we can map out what lies in the chapters ahead. The seven intensive care patients who died in a matter of months between May and September 2006 in a healthcare facility in the Czech Republic were not suffering from a terminal illness and were not in a great deal of pain; they were, in fact, expected to live. On December 1, Czech authorities arrested a 30-year-old male nurse; he'd been suspected at least three months earlier.

After the seventh patient died, Petr Zelenka was asked to resign from his position as a nurse at Havlickuv Brod Hospital, 60 miles southeast of Prague, a job in which he had been employed for the previous seven years. Despite growing suspicions, he was not fired; instead, his contract was renegotiated and he was free to leave. He moved on to yet another facility, getting new employment in healthcare on November 1. A month later, he was finally stopped and the community was shocked that he'd been allowed to move on.

Apparently the gathering of evidence was slow. A doctor had noticed as early as May that the facility seemed to have an unusually high number of cases of internal bleeding, and some of the patients died before the condition could be reversed. Zelenka, it turned out, was often part of the healthcare team for these patients. But when he went on vacation in August, the supposed epidemic of internal bleeding ceased. The hospital hoped it was just some strange occurrence, not to be repeated, but then Zelenka returned. In September, there were more such patient deaths.

He was asked to leave while an internal investigation ensued. It was found that Zelenka had been administering a blood-thinning drug, heparin, which in high doses can cause internal bleeding. Victims included both men and women, with all but one between the ages of 56 and 78. Apparently, he injected heparin from a hidden vial and would then complete his shift, aware that the patient was dying and waiting to see what would happen. Gambling on whether a doctor would step in to save the patient became a game to him—one in which he felt secretly smug. It's unlikely that his attitude would ever have been revealed had he not confessed it.

Initially after Zelenka's arrest, his motive for killing patients was unclear, but four days later when he confessed to 7 murders and 10 attempted murders, his attorney let it slip to reporters that Zelenka might have been injecting patients to test the doctors. His acts were supposedly impulsive and immature, based on a belief that the doctors at the hospital were not sufficiently skilled to figure out what was happening and stop it. Zelenka had apparently stated that using this drug in an overdose was a common mistake for staff people to make and an experienced doctor should have recognized it and applied the antidote. When patients died, Zelenka deduced that the facility's doctors weren't competent.

Reportedly, he was surprised to be caught, and this case caused a firestorm of criticism around the country. People could not fathom why a facility that suspected a nurse to be an outright killer could simply get rid of him instead of holding him to account for what he had done. That he had found work at yet another facility, without that facility being warned of the investigation into Zelenka's movements, was just as stunning. Apparently he did not have time to kill before being arrested, but critics believe he would have done so in short order. They argued that hospital administrators at his prior place of employment should have dealt more definitively with a nurse under suspicion of this nature.

But there was more to come. In January 2007, an expert commission that Health Minister Tomas Julinek had set up reported the results of its investigation; the committee had turned up five more suspicious deaths associated with Zelenka. Given what we have learned from HCSKs from the past, their initial confessions might not be truthful. In fact, we have reason to believe that one should always suspect the confession of a person long practiced in lies, deception, and murder. Psychopathic killers view their victims as objects, useful only as pawns in their game, and they thus have this advantage: they feel no remorse. Their sense of humanity is missing. They're callous, manipulative, and resistant to therapy, and when they choose to communicate, they have their own agendas, formed in self-interest. What we may accept as a confession, they might view as bait. Their motives form within a framework of calculation that has no equivalent in the normal world. Not even when they appear to be sincere.[4]

It's likely that this case will have an impact on healthcare policies in the Czech Republic, and similar cases in other countries have had similar reverberations. In the case of a HCSK, who operates within a system and might even be an indirect effect of the system's dysfunction, steps can be taken to close up the holes and prevent such occurrences in the future. Clarifying how these people operate should facilitate that process.

Before getting right to the HCSK phenomenon, we'll first examine historical healthcare killers, as well as examples of healthcare professionals who have committed murder but are not serial killers. Then we'll get right to the notorious doctors who have committed murder repeatedly, followed by the female and males nurses. Besides doctors and nurses, certain types of healthcare professionals also have access to patients, so chapter 6 discusses nurse's aides, therapists, and other healthcare-related occupations. We also have healthcare professionals who became serial killers *outside* the profession, as well as serial killers who falsely posed as doctors or nurses to engage the trust of their victims. Once the case details have been laid out, we can do a comprehensive analysis of what motivates these killers, and then discuss what healthcare communities can do when the right constellation of red flags identifies a potential killer. There are several experts around the world devoted specifically to the phenomenon of HCSKs, and their work proves useful for framing a means of understanding why healthcare workers kill and what can be done to try to reduce the incidents in the future.

1

Healthcare Killers vs. Healthcare Serial Killers

DUPLICITOUS DOCTOR

A young woman out walking in Moffat, Scotland, on a warm day in September 1935 leaned over the railing of a bridge and saw a cloth bundle snagged on a rock in the river Linn. Poking from the bundle was something that resembled a human arm. The woman ran for her brother, who fetched the police.

The object had indeed been an arm and a search produced three more packages containing more parts. While all proved to be female, the dismembered torso, arms, and legs weren't all from the same person. In fact, there were two heads. After an extensive search, the police collected some 60 pieces scattered over a wide terrain. A page of newsprint from the *Sunday Graphic* that was wrapped around two upper arms bore the date, September 15. It only remained to learn the identities of these murder victims.

The dismemberment was so precise that experts were convinced the killer was familiar with using a sharp carving knife: that indicated either a butcher or medical man. This person had been careful to skin the faces, remove the lips and noses, destroy the fingertips, and cut out the eyes from one and the teeth from both to make identification difficult. When the decomposing pieces were laid out, it was clear that one woman had been much older— about 40—and larger than the other. She had been beaten, stabbed five times, and strangled. Since the torso was missing for the younger woman, estimated to be around 20, it was difficult to tell what had happened to her, but the hands matched to her showed some printable areas on the fingertips, so her fingerprint impressions were taken.

The newspaper page helped detectives to pinpoint the probable area from which the corpses had originated, which coincided with the report from a local surgeon, Buck Ruxton, about his missing wife, 34. A known wife abuser, Ruxton was prone to insane fits of jealousy, so he became an immediate suspect. Investigators learned that Ruxton had informed the parents of his nursemaid, Mary Rogerson, age 20, that she had gotten pregnant so his wife had taken her to get an abortion. The parents did not believe him and against his wishes went to the police. So now they had two missing women whose description resembled the dismembered corpses.

Then more clues fell into place. The Rogersons identified a blouse wrapped around victim parts as their daughter's and a charwoman who worked for the Ruxtons reported that Dr. Ruxton had told her not to come on Sunday, September 15. The next day she had found the home in a mess, with unusual stains in the bath, carpets missing, and a pile of material burnt in the yard. Ruxton had given neighbors (who had helped him clean up the house) a bloody suit, claiming he had cut himself, and another neighbor saw him transporting a number of large bundles from his home. He gave out conflicting stories about his wife's absence, including that she had run off with another man.

What had occurred seemed clear: Ruxton had flown into a rage and beaten his wife to death. He then strangled and stabbed her, and young Mary might have run in at the wrong time, so she was killed, too. Ruxton cut them both into pieces in the bathtub (which yielded stains and traces of blood), wrapped the pieces in parcels, and threw them into the river, hoping no one could identify them should they wash ashore. On October 13, he was charged with two counts of murder. It did not take a jury long—an hour—to convict him. Before he was hanged on May 12, 1936, he wrote out a full confession.[1]

Ruxton's manner of committing and hiding the murders had revealed his intelligence and skill, although he had underestimated when the packages thrown in the river might be found. A physician's medical skill—especially that of a surgeon—is tantamount to a signature, assisting the police to narrow down the potential pool of suspects. Lots of men can stab and hack but only those skilled with a surgical knife can dismember with clean strokes. It might also be the case that Ruxton's education and skill had made him arrogant, thinking that he could persuade the family of one victim not to go to the police and that the charwoman would not be able to interpret the clues he'd left in the house. In fact, she did not until after the police had talked with her. If not for the newspapers he had used that helped the police to locate the right area, Ruxton might have gotten away with a double homicide.

CONVENIENCE

Hawley Harvey Crippen, too, killed and dismembered his wife, Cora, leaving town thereafter with his mistress, Ethel Le Neve. He was a patent salesman and homeopathic physician, residing with his wife at 30 Hilldrop Crescent in London. Small and seemingly mild-mannered, Crippen, 48, made a favorable impression on people, yet close acquaintances knew the couple was having problems. Then one day, Cora simply vanished without saying goodbye to a single friend. She had last been seen on January 31, 1910, and within a day Crippen was pawning some of her jewelry. He quickly moved his mistress into his home and told curious friends that Cora had gone to visit friends in America. It wasn't long before he said that she had grown ill and died there.

Le Neve took over the household and wore Cora's furs and jewelry. Cora's friends tried to get answers and finally contacted Scotland Yard, who sent Walter Dew to question Crippen. Dew searched Crippen's house and listened to his story, finding nothing to indicate foul play.

Yet in mid-January, Crippen had ordered five grains of hydrobromide of hyoscin at the shop of Lewis and Burrows—a considerable amount that demanded a special order and his signature. When police learned this, they remained suspicious, and when Crippen and his mistress suddenly left town, they returned to the house to search. Beneath bricks in the cellar they found a dismembered and decomposing torso wrapped in a pajama top. It was missing some organs, bones, and the genitals (all removed with surgical precision), and a tissue analysis indicated that this victim had ingested a lethal dose of hydrobromide of hyoscin. The pieces were coming together.

Although Crippen had attempted to flee aboard ship, he was detained and brought back to England. During his sensational murder trial, his counsel questioned that the remains were those of Crippen's wife, so two physicians identified a scar from the torso's lower abdomen as the result of a surgical procedure that Cora had received, as well as proving that the scar was not just a postmortem fold in the skin. After five days of testimony, the jury took 27 minutes to convict Crippen and he was hanged. (Ethel Le Neve was acquitted of any involvement.)[2]

Thus, as a physician, Crippen had utilized his legal access to a lethal amount of poison and then cut up his victim's body to the point where it was nearly unidentifiable. But a telling scar remained intact, and that, along with his strange stories and sudden flight in disguise, proved his undoing.

ELIMINATING A HINDRANCE

Another doctor devised a more cunning means of getting someone out of his way, and then used his reputation to deflect suspicion. This doctor's victim, in fact, was a close friend, and it took several decades before the crime was even identified as such. On June 2, 1976, in Montrose, Pennsylvania, Dr. Stephen Scher went out with lawyer Martin Dillon to shoot clay pigeons. Only Scher returned home, because Dillon was dead.

They'd been walking to get some cigarettes, Scher stated, when Dillon had spotted a porcupine, grabbed Scher's Winchester 16-guage pump-action shotgun, ran after the animal, and then tripped, falling onto the gun. It went off and killed him. Scher, who said he was about 250 feet away, ran to him. When he turned Dillon over, he saw a gaping chest wound that, as a doctor, he knew was fatal. Since Dillon's shoe lacings were undone, Scher surmised that he'd stepped on one. Scher was so overcome, he averred, that he'd smashed the gun against a tree, thereby rendering it useless for a ballistics test.

Since the two men had both been close acquaintances of the district attorney, and the facts appeared to support Scher's explanation, the death was declared accidental. Aside from an autopsy in which the pathologist described Dillon's wound as a contact wound, there was no further investigation. However, Dillon's father, Lawrence Dillon, believed that his son had not died by accident. His suspicions were further strengthened when two years following the incident, Scher married Dillon's widow, Pat. She had worked with Scher and prior to the incident had been rumored to be having an affair with him. As town mayor, Lawrence Dillon pressured for an investigation, but resistance from other officials was strong. He bided his time.

In 1992, Lawrence Dillon hired a private detective to review the evidence. It turned out that there was blood spatter on Scher's clothing and boots, along with a piece of flesh pierced by fibers on his pants—evidence that he had been standing much closer to Dillon than he'd admitted—in fact quite close. Dr. Isadore Mihalakis, a coroner and forensic pathologist from another county, agreed to re-examine the case.

He looked at the death scene photo and wondered how, if Dillon had been running, his pants legs were hiked up and the lacing of his boots were still tight against his legs, despite being untied. Running would have loosened them. The coroner also noted from photos taken at the scene that a clay pigeon was near to Dillon's hand, as if dropped. It made little sense that he'd have carried it while running to shoot an animal. These facts undermined Scher's story, so Mihalakis decided to exhume Dillon to measure his arm length and compare it to the reach for the shotgun's trigger. In the process, they would re-examine the wound.

It turned out that Dillon could have reached the trigger, but the gun muzzle would have been very close to him. Yet there was no blackening around the wound to indicate a close-range shot. However, there were tiny pellet markings, so investigators tried several experiments, the end result of which was to prove that Scher had lied about what had occurred. There was no shotgun powder on Dillon's arm, as there should have been, but there was blood spatter on his trousers, which would not have resulted from the gun's alleged angle.

The investigators' conclusion was that the muzzle of the shotgun that had killed Dillon had been at least three and a half feet away, and his wound angle indicated that he was shot from above. In addition, a fine mist of blood on Dillon's boots suggested that he'd been sitting or crouching when shot. The death was thus declared a homicide, staged to look like an accident, and Dr. Scher was arrested and brought to trial.

He confessed that he had indeed shot Dillon but insisted it had been accidental as they argued and then fought over the gun. However, since Dillon was wearing earplugs when found, Scher's claim rang hollow. In 1997, Scher was convicted of first-degree murder and sentenced to life in prison. Two years later, he was released on appeal, but in 2002, the Pennsylvania Supreme Court upheld the conviction and Scher returned to prison.[3]

Apparently, as a physician, Scher had believed that he knew well enough how to stage a homicide to look like an accidental death. Certainly he'd seen plenty of shooting incidents in his practice in northeastern Pennsylvania. He'd also apparently been sufficiently confident of himself to kill the husband of a woman with whom he was believed to be having an affair and then to marry her afterward. Such are the hallmarks of physicians who decide to cross the line from healer to killer. They view themselves as untouchable.

COPYCAT SLAUGHTER

A doctor who was convicted of killing his pregnant wife and two daughters, then staging the scene to look like the work of deranged hippie intruders, was Dr. Jeffrey MacDonald. While the conviction has long been controversial and the evidence against him challenged, at this writing he remains in prison for the crimes. In part, it was his behavior after the triple homicide that did him in, because it was his own father-in-law, who once had sided with him, who finally grew suspicious. Although this case might be questionable, it's worth a brief review of the reasons the jury found MacDonald guilty, since it appears that his professional expertise was a factor.

On February 17, 1970, the military police at Fort Bragg answered a distress call from the home of Dr. Jeffrey MacDonald. When they arrived, the place was dark and they found him lying on the floor of his master bedroom, wounded, while his murdered family was sprawled all over the house. Colette MacDonald, his 26-year-old pregnant wife, had been stabbed numerous times in the chest, and she lay bludgeoned and bleeding in the bedroom underneath a torn blue pajama top. Written in blood on the headboard of the bed was the word, *Pig*. Down the hall in one bedroom was two-year-old Kristen, stabbed 33 times, and her sister Kimberly, age five, also repeatedly stabbed.

In comparison to the attacks on the females, MacDonald's wounds were relatively minor and as police searched the house he told them what he could recall: he'd been sleeping on the living room couch when Colette's cries woke him. Three men and a woman, dressed like hippies, had invaded his home, chanting about LSD. MacDonald tried to fight them, using his pajama top to defend himself, but they slashed him with an ice pick and knocked him unconscious with a baseball bat. When he revived, he discovered his wife and daughters dead, so he made the emergency call.

Detectives William Ivory and Franz Grebner found that MacDonald's story failed to add up. The relatively minor disorder in the living room was inconsistent with the struggle he'd described, but more suspicious was the fact that a magazine on the table contained extensive coverage of the recent stabbing murders attributed to the Charles Manson gang in California. The incident looked staged, especially since MacDonald himself should have taken the brunt of the frenzy, since he was most likely the hated "pig." It was also disturbing that MacDonald, who reportedly had terrible eyesight without his glasses, had been able to give such detailed descriptions of the perpetrators in his home. And why had he dialed the phone in the dark? Or if he'd had the light on, why had he turned it off again before the police arrived?

Then other evidence emerged. On the bed where Colette had been attacked was the torn finger from a latex glove such as surgeons wear, and a knife that MacDonald claimed to have pulled out of his wife was clean of fingerprints… even his. It also proved not to be the knife that had stabbed Colette. Also free of prints were both of the phones that MacDonald said he'd used to call for help. Even more troubling was the fact that several blue threads from the pajama top were found beneath Colette, although MacDonald said that he'd laid the garment on top of her. Quite a few fibers were discovered below the headboard of the bed where the word *pig* had been written by the finger of a right-handed person wearing something that resembled a glove. More fibers turned up on a bloodstained piece of wood found in the backyard, where police found an ice pick and another knife, both wiped clean. Blue threads also turned up in the children's bedrooms, including one under Kristen's fingernail, but none were present in the room where MacDonald claimed he was sleeping—where the jacket had supposedly been torn.

The most damning evidence, according to the prosecution, was the blood pattern analysis. Each family member had a different blood group, which made it possible to track where they had been. MacDonald's blood showed up in the kitchen next to a cabinet that contained surgical gloves. It was also in the bathroom, but there was none in the living room where he'd claimed to have been stabbed, except for a tiny smear on a magazine. A footprint in Kristen's bedroom was made with Colette's blood. Added to all of this was the lack of evidence that four intruders had not only entered the house but had struggled with all of the victims. Hair from a wig was perhaps the most controversial item, because it supported the story about a woman in a wig being with the hippies.

FBI analyst Paul Stombaugh examined MacDonald's pajama top and observed that all 48 holes made by the ice pick had smooth edges and a round shape. He believed that this could only have occurred if the garment had been stationary. Stombaugh then folded the jacket to see how the stab marks matched and was able to show that the 48 punctures could have been made by 21 thrusts of the pick, which matched the number of stab wounds found on Colette's body. (This is one of the items of evidence under vigorous dispute.)

MacDonald was convicted of one count of first-degree murder and two counts of two second-degree murders, and he is currently serving three consecutive life terms. He stands as a doctor whom a jury believed had used his surgical skill to fatally stab his entire family and then inflict non-lethal cuts on himself.[4]

But not all such killers are doctors, and they're also not always self-serving and intentionally homicidal.

TOUGH CALL

Three days after Hurricane Katrina devastated New Orleans in August of 2005, shutting down all systems and paralyzing hospitals, staff members of all healthcare facilities faced difficult decisions about what to do with dying patients. At the city's Memorial Medical Center, several healthcare professionals discussed euthanasia as an option, although no one wanted to do this unless all other avenues were exhausted. Still, there was no rescue in sight, the city had no water or power, hundreds of people were dying in the streets, and those who remained were in fear for their own lives.

Finally, the tough decisions were made, and those who acted to euthanize five patients reportedly prayed with them and made them as comfortable as possible before giving them overdoses of morphine. Some who participated worried over whether God would forgive them, but they also knew these patients would never make it out of the sweltering, crime-ridden city, which faced even more bad weather. This act seemed to them preferable to leaving the patients in agony, begging for help.

When the story came to light months later, Dr. Anna Pou and two nurses, Cheri Landry and Lori Budo, were arrested in July 2006 and charged as principals to second-degree murder. Their case is still pending, but the dismal situation they faced required decisions that medical personnel would not ordinarily face. While some people call these patients victims of medical murder, and it might be decided thus in a court of law, it's clear that the act of mercy performed was not motivated by personal gain, anger, or predatory thrill. The desperate nature of the act, and the attempt to assist patients not to suffer through the hardship of starvation or dehydration, places this situation of medical homicide in a category all its own.[5]

In a study that involved 852 nurses practicing in adult intensive care units, 19 percent admitted to having participated in some form of euthanasia. Only 30 percent of the nurses who confessed believed the practice is unethical. Although at times, when a patient was critically ill, and a nurse had decided against carrying out a physician's orders so as to hasten a patient's death, it was usually the patient or patient's family who made the request. This quiet practice is quite different from the methods and motives attributed to nurses who kill patients for personal reasons or decide on the patient's behalf that he or she should die.[6]

Euthanasia aside, there are many cases throughout history of doctors and nurses who have killed only once. Such professionals are psychologically different from the healthcare worker who becomes a serial killer, and this difference must be analyzed, because they would not be considered predators. Greedy, perhaps, and even despicable in some circumstances, but not predatory in terms of repeatedly seeking to target and kill acquaintances or strangers. Nevertheless, some have been utterly cold-blooded.

HOMICIDAL NURSES

On October 27, 2001, a battered male body was discovered in a park in Fort Worth, Texas. Thirty-seven-year-old Gregory Biggs appeared to have been the victim of a hit-and-run, but four months later, a bizarre story emerged. It seems that as a woman named Chante Mallard drove home one night under the influence of drugs and alcohol, she struck Biggs. While initially, this was indeed an accident, her subsequent actions shifted it into the category of intentional murder.

Detectives searched Mallard's home and found her Chevrolet Cavalier, clearly damaged, still in her garage. But someone had tried to hide or remove evidence. The windshield had been mostly knocked out and a seat removed. Blood spatters inside the car were from Biggs, as was the blood that filled a side-door pocket compartment. In addition, a hammer left in the backseat was proven with trace analysis to have been used against glass, an indication of evidence tampering. It all added up to a man struggling and bleeding substantially in that space.

The medical examiner who'd conducted the autopsy stated that none of the injuries was consistent with instantaneous death, so with medical assistance Biggs could have survived. Mallard, a nurse's aid, had sufficient expertise to have saved him, and she certainly knew whom to call for help. She admitted that, although stuck, Biggs had been moaning and moving around. But touching him had scared her.

The crime reconstruction indicated that as Mallard hit Biggs, he came through her windshield headfirst and lodged there, his arms pinned to his sides. She then drove eight miles to her house and parked in her garage, leaving Biggs struggling and bleeding in the windshield. As he expired over the course of an hour or two, Mallard checked him and actually apologized. When she found him dead, she and two male friends dumped him in the park. Mallard, a member of the helping profession, was convicted of murder and sentenced to 50 years, with another 10-year sentence for evidence tampering.[7]

Some male nurses, too, have been guilty of outright homicide in a context other than healthcare. The trial of Gary Earl Leiterman began July 11, 2005. Via a DNA analysis, the former nurse was charged with the 1969 murder of University of Michigan law student Jane Mixer, 23, who had disappeared after accepting a ride as she attempted to get home for the weekend. The next day, her body was found in a cemetery, fully dressed, with a coat placed protectively over her. She had been shot twice in the head with a .22. She also had a stocking tied around her neck.

Leiterman was now 62. His DNA had been included in the FBI's national database after a conviction for prescription fraud. When biological stains from Mixer's pantyhose were tested against that same database, they hit on Leiterman. The odds that it had come from a Caucasian man other than Leiterman were calculated at 170 trillion to one, despite his outright denial. Then a documents expert said that a phrase, "Muskegon—Mixer," found penned in a phone book in 1969 was most likely Leiterman's handwriting, although another expert contradicted this. Leiterman had owned a .22 hand-gun at the time of Mixer's death, but he reported it stolen in 1987, so it could not be fired for comparison tests. A merchant testified that Leiterman had purchased .22-caliber ammunition in February, just a month before Mixer's death. How Leiterman came across Mixer was not known, but investigators assumed he had noticed her ad for a ride and arranged to pick her up.

The two-week trial ended with a quick verdict: Leiterman was found guilty of first-degree murder and received life in prison. He continued to deny his guilt.[8]

We can conclude that most medical professionals who resort to one-time, situational murder, which would probably not be repeated, initiate such acts outside the context of their workplace. It's generally some issue in their per-sonal lives that contributes to the situation, or perhaps even a compulsion that they generally kept hidden, but they tend to rely on their training and familiarity with medicine, handling of patients, and proximity to death to work up the courage to accomplish the act and dispose of the victim. At the very least, it seems that handling a corpse does not disturb them.

Let's move on to the men and women who become serial killers, starting with some of the most infamous cases from the past.

2

Historic Angels of Death

THE UNLIKELY CRIMINAL

During the mid- to late-nineteenth century, anthropologists had proposed theories, accepted by the masses, that there was a so-called criminal type, and that he had a fairly obvious appearance—thuggish and simian. Thus, the well-to-do, educated, and so-called normal appearing man was usually considered safe—and if he actually wasn't safe, he had an advantage. It was easy for him to elicit trust, especially if he was in a care-taking profession.

During these times, a physician who used his medical skills to kill, Dr. William Palmer, came to the attention of British authorities. Because he gambled on horse races, he was ever in need of money to pay his debts, and when several people around him unexpectedly expired, he was arrested. In 1855, Palmer was accused of using strychnine to poison a friend named John Parsons Cook, who had died and who Palmer said left him a considerable sum. In fact, Palmer had asked another doctor for some strychnine shortly before this death and had forged a check to himself, supposedly from Cook. Because Palmer was a doctor, he'd been allowed to attend the autopsy on Cook and he somehow surreptitiously picked up a jar into which the surgeon had put the contents of the dead man's stomach. But Palmer did not get far—not even out of the room—and his actions supported suspicions of his involvement in the death. Although no strychnine was found, Palmer remained in jail on other charges, and his career as a poisoner and thief was soon to end. In some ways, there is little wonder that he chose this means to pay his debts.

In Palmer's background was a con artist: his mother's father had made the family wealthy by seducing and slowly defrauding a wealthy widow until she had no more money. In addition, Palmer's father had grown successful off the theft of timber. William was born in 1824 and proved to be a bright but lazy child. His apprenticeship to a chemist introduced him to the world of drugs and poisons, but as a teenager he developed into an alcoholic, womanizer, and gambler. In 1846, William qualified as a doctor and was rumored to have poisoned the husband of a woman he was wooing.

Over the course of several years, as he fathered at least 15 illegitimate children, Palmer was associated with a string of other unexpected deaths, including those of his well-insured wife, an illegitimate child whom he declined to support, several relatives and associates, and his mother-in-law. A few of these people had died quite suddenly while in Palmer's home. He'd even insured his own brother, Walter, and invited him into a bout of drinking, whereupon Walter expired. The insurance company refused to pay for this death, so Palmer insured someone else, who also quickly died. After the death of John Parsons Cook, suspicious investigators decided to exhume some of the deceased, and in Palmer's wife's remains, they discovered a large dose of antinomy, a fatal poison.

The circumstantial evidence surrounding Cook's death and the forgeries that Palmer had committed to fraudulently acquire money did him in, and he was convicted and then hanged in 1856. In a bit of poetic justice, the rope for his noose was cut into pieces and sold for a healthy profit. In the end, it was suspected that Palmer had murdered at least 12 people.[1] (Ironically, the doctor who acted as a toxicology expert went on to kill his three wives and then himself, before he could be hanged.)

Later that same century, another doctor found some satisfaction in the art of murder, and he became a suspect in the series of killings in 1888 in London that were attributed to Jack the Ripper (considered by some experts to have been a surgeon).

THE SKILL TO KILL

Thomas Neill Cream was born in Glasgow in 1850 but raised in Quebec, Canada. Because his unusual intelligence was obvious as he became a young man, his parents sent him to a university and by 1876, Cream was a doctor. He was also a con artist and arsonist. One day, a young chambermaid named Kate Gardner was found dead in a privy with a bottle of chloroform next to her. She was soon linked to Cream, an abortionist, but after he managed to avoid prosecution, he moved on to Chicago. When a girl died there, Cream was arrested, but again officials declined to make him answer for what he had probably done. Next he poisoned the husband of a beautiful patient with whom he was carrying on a relationship, and inexplicably informed the police that they should exhume the man and look for strychnine, which he blamed on the chemist who had supplied it. Apparently he just wanted someone to realize that a murder had been committed, which gave him some sort of perverse secret pleasure, but his plan backfired and he was convicted and sentenced to prison. After his release 10 years later, Cream ended up in England in 1891, moving to South London.

By this time, the five murders attributed to Jack the Ripper remained unsolved, but the police were still actively seeking the perpetrator. All of the victims had been prostitutes, and all were slaughtered in a particularly brutal manner, with their throats slit. The killer had walked off with parts of their organs as well. The police continued to monitor prostitute murders there-after, in case they found another to link to this spree. It seemed in 1891 that the killings had resumed.

Cream relied on strychnine to slay several young prostitutes. He then brought attention to the murders by writing strange notes to various officials, signed with pseudonyms. However, in one letter he revealed key details about a murder that few people knew, so the police believed these notes had come from the killer. They kept them together in the event they could acquire a handwriting sample from a suspect. They did wonder if there was any rela-tionship to Red Jack, although these women had been poisoned not stabbed. Nevertheless, they were prostitutes.

Oddly, Cream befriended one of the lead detectives from Scotland Yard—perhaps playing a dangerous game—and offered information he had heard about the murders that failed to check out. Thus, rather than deflecting the investigation as he seemed to intend, he attracted it. He was asked for an account of himself since he'd been in England, and his handwriting matched that in the letters—missives that had been written on American-made paper. Since Cream had recently traveled to New York, this proved to be one more suggestive factor against him. He falsely claimed that his bag contained drug samples from a company he represented, but the presence of strychnine in an exhumed victim with whom Cream was seen before she died sealed his fate.

Arrested in 1892 for one of the murders, Cream was convicted and sen-tenced to be hanged. By some accounts, as the hangman drew the bolt, Cream allegedly announced, "I am Jack the—" as the noose broke his neck. Since he was in prison during the Ripper's spree in White Chapel, it's likely that he hoped to become famous by associating himself with Red Jack, because he had nothing to lose by it. While we can't be certain, it's suspected that Cream had killed at least eight people, including a man, and in each instance he used his medical knowledge to do so.[2]

The same can be said of the next murdering physician, although he had many more victims.

SWINDLING, SHAM, AND SLAUGHTER

Whenever there has been a formal practice of medicine and people who knew how to use the medical arts to heal, there have also been those who spotted the opportunity to exploit these same methods to kill. Among the most notorious historical serial killers is a man who even faked his name.

Herman Webster Mudgett was born in New Hampshire in 1860. As he grew into a young man, he became fascinated with dissection and surgery. To assuage his curiosity, he would catch animals to kill and perform anatomical experiments. After he turned 18, he attended medical school at the University of Michigan, where he learned how to make money via medical fraud.

Mudgett stole corpses to practice experiments and eventually realized that his comfort around the dead allowed him to use them however he pleased, which grew into defrauding life insurance companies. He would take out policies using fictitious names, obliterate the features of a cadaver with acid, and tell the companies that the cadaver was the deceased. Eventually Mudgett was caught and banned from his place of employment, so he moved on to Englewood, Illinois, a suburb of Chicago.

There he abandoned his name, reinventing himself as Dr. Henry Howard Holmes. He soon persuaded a widow who owned a pharmacy to let him work for her as a druggist, and it wasn't long before she disappeared. Holmes then used the thriving business to sell fake cures, which made him wealthy. Though married already, he married again, and would continue to do so, sometimes killing these women to enrich himself.

With his new funds, Holmes set a fiendish fantasy into motion. He built a three-story hotel to let rooms to tourists, which coincided nicely with the 1893 Chicago World's Fair, but he included secret soundproof chambers for his own entertainment. Certain attractive young women who checked in alone were often booked into these rooms, which locked and let in lethal gas. Holmes would watch through a peephole as they died from asphyxiation or might even ignite the gas to incinerate them, and then he'd slide their bodies via hidden chutes into the cellar. Down there, he would dismember their corpses on a dissecting table and them dump them into vats of acid or burn them in the oversized furnace. Then he'd sell the bleached skeletons to medical schools.

At one point, Holmes hired a lackey, Herman Pitezel, to oversee his construction and run errands. Pitezel knew what Holmes was doing and he agreed to take out a life insurance policy on himself. He and Holmes planned to find a suitable corpse to perpetrate the fraud and then split the proceeds. But Holmes then smothered his would-be accomplice with chloroform and burned him alive with acid. He set fire to the laboratory where Pitezel's corpse lay to make it look like an accident and the next day used Pitezel's oldest daughter to identify the body. From that mishap, he pocketed $10,000. Then he persuaded Pitezel's wife and family to escape with him, convincing them that the corpse the authorities had found was not Pitezel. He eventually killed three of the five children, burning the boy in a stove in a rented home and burying the girls in the cellar of yet another place in Canada.

However, Holmes had neglected to split the proceeds with a third accomplice, and that man, sitting in prison for another crime, alerted the insurance company to the fraud. Pitezel's death was re-examined as a murder and the police set out after Holmes. They grabbed him in Massachusetts and charged him with murder. Despite bragging about his criminal career, Holmes insisted he was innocent. He remained in prison while an intrepid detective located the bodies of the missing Pitezel children.

Investigators in Chicago soon discovered several complete skeletons and numerous bone fragments in the Chicago hotel, but Holmes insisted that he had nothing to do with them. Those people had either taken their own lives, he claimed, or been killed by someone else. While he sat in his cell, he wrote a book to explain how he was innocent of all the charges. He then tried to defend himself at his trial, but was woefully inadequate. On November 4, 1895, Holmes/Mudgett was convicted of the first-degree murder of Herman Pitezel.

Finally, inspired by payment from the Hearst newspaper syndicate, Holmes penned a gruesome confession for *The Philadelphia Inquirer*, insisting it had been his aim to become the most notorious murderer in the world, a killer of monstrous proportions. He estimated that he had killed over one hundred people. Having second thoughts, he brought that number down to 27 and claimed that he could not help but do what he'd done. "I was born with the Evil One as my sponsor beside the bed where I was ushered into the world," he lamented.[3]

Then he recanted the confession, and in fact it turned out that several of his alleged victims were not dead at all. Yet so many people who'd rented rooms from him had gone missing that estimates of his true victims reached around 200. In truth, no one knows the actual number.

On May 7, 1896, Holmes was taken to the hangman's noose, and even there he claimed to have killed only two women. Once again, he was lying.

Only a decade later, a female physician used another deceptive means to claim her victims.

DEATH BY FASTING

Among the few female physicians who have committed a murder, and this one in the context of healthcare, was Linda Burfield Hazzard. She set up a healthcare facility during the early 1900s for wealthy people who were seeking methods to ensure their health. The fad at this time was to go to some sort of retreat facility and submit oneself to the rigors of whatever therapy was currently in vogue. Sometimes such spas offered genuine service but often they were full of quackery, poised simply to siphon off money from trusting clients.

Dr. Hazzard set up her operation in 1907 in Seattle, Washington, and offered several versions of a published manual that outlined her special method. One of the few female doctors in the United States at this time (trained as an osteopath), Hazzard presented herself as the only licensed fasting therapist in the country. Her ultimate domain for this elite treatment was a sanitarium, Wilderness Heights, in the small town of Olalla, across the Puget Sound from Seattle. It was an isolated place, with no way to communicate with the outside world. Once a person signed in, there were few ways to contact anyone on the outside or to get back out.

Exuding self-confidence, Dr. Hazzard assured people who came to check out her facility that her method was a panacea for all manner of ills, because she was able to rid the body of toxins that caused physiological imbalances. As strange as it may seem, she managed to persuade people to accept her premise, to sign themselves over to her, and to go entirely without food for long periods, aside from some water and a thin tomato and asparagus soup. As their bodies shed these so-called toxins, Hazzard required her patients to submit to regular enemas (a fashionable purgative in many such places) and she and her small staff provided vigorous massages meant to accelerate the process.

Dr. Hazzard apparently had something else in mind besides her patients' well-being, and as they weakened, they became vulnerable to her other requirements. Hazzard encouraged her patients, mostly females, to turn over to her their accounts and their power of attorney. Her bigamous husband, Sam, helped get the patients to change their wills to name Dr. Hazzard their beneficiary. Not surprisingly, several of these patients died at her facility and she grew richer. News of these deaths reached the mainland, inspiring a public reaction, but when attacked for her methods, Hazzard insisted that these patients had been near death when they came; she could not be expected to work miracles. Even with these dire stories, Hazzard managed to attract both disciples and willing patients from around the world.

Not surprisingly, local residents dubbed the place Starvation Heights, and it finally came to the attention of authorities after two wealthy British heiresses endured the supposed cure. Claire and Dora Williamson had received a copy of *Fasting for the Cure of Disease,* reading about how Dr. Hazzard had cured many people who had found no other help for their conditions. While the tales and testimonials were impressive, they were impossible to check for validity. Potential patients such as the Williamson sisters, who had no medical background, tended to be gullible as well as eager to be among the success stories. Fans of natural remedies, the Williamsons checked in on February 27, 1911.

The sisters both agreed to undergo the rigorous fasting regimen and they began to shed weight at a rapid rate. In fact, photos of them show that they resembled some of the extreme images today of anorexia nervosa patients. Naturally, they weakened, but given how Hazzard had documented these symptoms as indications that they were actually growing healthier, they renewed their commitment to the program. Even the suffering they endured while starving, they were told, was a sign that the treatment was working.

After two months of this fasting cure, both sisters took to their beds and were hardly able to move. Still, the doctor did not allow them to eat. While they were feeling ill and even delirious, Hazzard secured their jewelry and land deeds, to, as she said, "prevent others" from coming into their apartment to rob them. Then she moved them to her newly completed sanitarium, where they could literally communicate with no one. At that time, they weighed around 75 pounds each—far too little for a grown woman. In fact, in this state they weren't far from death's door.

Claire managed to surreptitiously find a worker on the grounds to send a telegram to her faithful childhood nanny, Martha Convey, who rushed there by ship from Australia. Convey was too late; Claire had already died, but Convey did rescue Dora, now nearly psychotic from starvation. The nanny also saw to it that Dr. Hazzard was arrested for the murder of Claire Williamson.

With Convey's nurturing, Dora regained her health, so she was ready when Hazzard's trial occurred in 1912. The photos taken of her after four months of the treatment were in stark contrast with how she looked in the courtroom, and when she added that the jewels she had taken to the sanitarium were missing, as well as describing the prison-like conditions, the case against Hazzard was convincing. Yet without remorse, Hazzard apparently joked with one reporter that they wouldn't be able to hang her because her neck muscles were too strong. She insisted she was innocent.

The jury found Hazzard guilty of manslaughter, and newspapers at the time indicated that her gender had probably saved her from a murder verdict. Dora wept when she heard, but Hazzard insisted she was a victim and swore that she would right the injustice done to her.

During her legal proceedings, to protect society the Washington State Board of Medical Examiners removed her license. Undaunted, Hazzard claimed that the verdict was part of the persecution she had suffered all along for her revolutionary ideas especially from the educated. As evidence, she cited the fact that the judge had barred patients who had benefited from her treatment from testifying on her behalf. Her attorney appealed.

During this process, her sanitarium continued to operate under other management, and two more women, as well as two babies, died there. These patients had entered the treatment after the trial and were apparently unfazed by the conviction. Hazzard spent only two years in prison, and in exchange for her leaving the country the state governor granted a pardon. Hazzard took her operation to New Zealand for a while, but eventually returned to Olalla to resume her business. Arrested again when another man died, she was fined for violating medical practice. Since she kept no records, the number of people who died (or were intentionally starved to death) cannot be estimated. Ironically, when Hazzard took ill in 1938, she fasted herself to death. The sanitarium eventually burned to the ground.[4]

At the same time, another doctor was already in killing mode in France.

PLAYING BOTH SIDES

A man who exploited wartime conditions in Paris to deceive and kill people for his own enrichment, was Dr. Marcel Petiot. He had a knack for getting people to trust him and legal access to the means to kill them, one after another.

Born in 1897 in Auxerre, France, Petiot was an orphan by the time he reached puberty. One of his aunts begrudgingly raised him, so he experienced early in life how to emotionally detach himself as a way to survive. Two major losses and the lack of significant caretakers would affect how he conducted business. In fact, he was apparently not easy to like at any age, developing a certain cruelty that urged him into sadistic acts. He enjoyed hurting animals, although he sometimes showed remorse—or apparent remorse, as he developed the ability to act one way yet be someone else altogether; but he kept his secrets.

When he was 18, Petiot became a registered medical student, but only a year later in 1916 he was drafted into the army. World War I was in full swing in the trenches that stretched across northern Europe, and Petiot became a medical orderly on the field of battle. However, that career, too, was cut short when a live grenade wounded his hand. It wasn't long before he ended up under psychiatric care, which he firmly resisted. Eventually, he persuaded authorities to return him to his unit. What he really wanted, apparently, was his easy access as a medical person to drugs, which he quickly sold to addicts. For this activity, Petiot received a court martial. His prior mental instability mitigated the offense and he was ordered to get more treatment. He went to a facility in Rennes for two years before returning home to continue treatment as an outpatient.

The time off from the army had provided the opportunity to continue to study medicine and Petiot soon became a doctor, writing a thesis on hereditary paralysis. In 1924, he set up a practice in Villeneuve, about 70 miles south of Paris. He even became its mayor by the following year, and his medical practice was a striking success—despite a social scandal in his household.

It seems that a young girl who came to be Petiot's housekeeper ended up pregnant. She then vanished. The police received an anonymous letter that Petiot had murdered her, but an investigation turned up no evidence, so no arrest was made. Petiot soon married a woman named Georgette Lablais, from a wealthy family, and they had a son.

Petiot did get caught for one criminal act: he was stealing electricity for his surgery. For this he received a suspended sentence. Still, he lost his position as mayor, but then he was subsequently re-elected. This psychopath seemed always to slip through the system unscathed, or with very little punishment. The townspeople liked him and forgave his various transgressions—including more thefts. But they did not forgive his apparent connection with a murder—the strangulation death of a woman who ran a dairy. A witness had spotted Petiot leaving the scene of the crime. But soon that person, a patient of Petiot's, died suddenly of natural causes, or so said Petiot, the attending doctor.

Pressured to resign as mayor, Petiot eventually made his way to Paris—a city in which he would not be quite as visible. He set up his practice at 66 rue Caumartin, in the commercially developed ninth arrondissement, making house calls via motorcycle. Once again, he had no trouble developing a thriving practice, and his easy success gave him confidence to test the law, but he was arrested for stealing books. Again using the excuse of his past mental instability, Petiot convinced a doctor to send him for treatment rather than to prison. At no time during this latest scandal was his permit to practice medicine withdrawn.

Then, as the result of a significant defeat for the Allies at the Battle of France near the Belgian border, the French government signed an armistice that allowed the Germans to occupy northern and western regions of France, including Paris. The rest of France was run by the French government at Vichy. At this time, in mid-1940, Petiot purchased an impressive estate on the rue LeSuere near the Arch de Triomphe, although it was not for his family. He altered it for his own secret purposes, including a substantial privacy wall. Inside, he devised a bricked-up room, triangular in shape, and drilled a small hole through one wall. Petiot also had a hole dug beneath the floor of the garage and he brought in a large boiler. He told acquaintances he hoped to turn the place into a psychiatric facility, so he could specialize in diseases of the mind.

The Germans, with the French puppet government, set up new rules in occupied France, which included the death penalty for specific types of crimes, notably abortion. Petiot, however, built a thriving practice by offering this service, alongside his pastime of supplying drugs to addicts. When one woman's procedure started rumors around her village, she approached Petiot for a means to cover it up, but then she disappeared. Apparently he was not keen on publicity of any kind. Others who threatened to expose the doctor similarly disappeared. For all anyone knew, given the wartime conditions, they had escaped France or been arrested by the Gestapo.

In 1942, Petiot devised his most fiendish means of self-enrichment, which also allowed him to experiment on people. Jews were being herded into ghettos and camps in other countries, so it seemed but a matter of time before Jews in France would suffer the same fate. Many were looking for ways to leave. Petiot assured those who confided in him that he was a member of the underground Resistance movement and could help. If they could pay the bribe money he would need, he said, he could get them out of the country. Many Jews handed their valuables and large sums of money to Petiot. In addition, as per his instructions, they had removed from their person any identification.

Petiot assured the relatives and friends of these people that they were well on their way overseas, although they had never left. But in light of the uncertainty of the times and the difficulty of getting mail through, no one could be certain what had happened to those from whom they never heard again. Petiot did make the mistake of offering a similar deal to members of the criminal underworld, and when one was caught he told the Gestapo about Petiot's refugee business. But Petiot, clever man that he was, had a ready story. Knowing how the German military hated Jews, he said that, contrary to rumors, he was not really helping them escape but was killing them. Thus, he was assisting Hitler's plan. The Germans detained him to check this out, but eventually released him. In fact, he had told the truth, although his so-called work was hardly on behalf of the Third Reich, and he returned to it at once.

Petiot's modus operandi regarding victims was to tell them he had to give them an injection against typhoid. They willingly allowed him to administer his poison, and he then locked them up and watched through his peephole as they died. But the more he killed, the more bodies he had, which proved to be a problem. Since he had a rather grand furnace, he dismembered and stuffed the bodies into it, burning the parts mostly at night. Then, greedy for all he could acquire, on March 11, 1944, he placed too many corpses into the fire at once and left the premises on business. The fire burned out of control and the stench that spread throughout the neighborhood was terrible. The fire brigade responded, along with the French police, and it did not take these officials long to see that significant crimes had been committed on these premises.

Near the furnace in the basement were dismembered human limbs—arms and legs—and a pile of torsos. But once again, Petiot had a story. This time he was back on the side of the Resistance and he claimed that the bodies in the basement were German soldiers and French collaborators—enemies of, or traitors to, France. He then managed to walk away, but an investigation of the estate turned up clothing, valuables, and property from many people stashed into the various rooms. Some items belonged to children, and most of the names on a list found in one room were Jewish.

The Paris newspapers immediately published stories about Petiot's sinister business, although Petiot and his family were nowhere to be found. He was still in Paris, in disguise. He went undiscovered for several months, as the Allies freed France from German control in August 1944.

Then a letter arrived to a newspaper, praising Petiot as a French hero, and a handwriting analysis indicated that Petiot himself had written it. A check with higher ranking officials in the Resistance identified a recent recruit as the fugitive. By November, he was once again in police custody, but this time they weren't as gullible. The investigation was thorough, lasting a year and a half, and Petiot was tried in March 1946 for 27 provable murders. He was suspected in many more.

Petiot continued to tell the story that his victims were traitors or enemies, and attempted to beguile the jury as he had charmed so many other people throughout his life. However, since no person whom he had supposedly assisted to escape ever returned or contacted a relative, and since many people were able to identify possessions from their missing loved ones, Petiot had little ground on which to stand. No one in the Resistance had ever heard of him either, and none condoned his methods. The jury was unimpressed with Petiot's bluster, so they took about two hours to convict him of 24 of the murders. He was executed on May 26, 1946.[5]

The Germans, too, had their wartime medical executioners. In fact, quite a few doctors participated in Hitler's attempt to wipe out what he perceived as undesirable populations, but one stands out as the epitome of evil.

THE ARYAN PRACTITIONER

He was genial and even paternal with the very children he expected to either deform or exterminate. A proponent of biomedical experimentation, he viewed them all as canvases on which to paint, nothing more. He even gave out candy and let his intended victims ride in his car—straight to their deaths. But there was no mistaking his approach: Joseph Mengele thought only of his work and his own ambitions. These children of Jews and other supposedly objectionable types of people were considered expendable. He decided that they existed solely for his benefit and the betterment of the Aryan race; he could do whatever he liked, even if that included terrible suffering for the child.

Mengele arrived in Auschwitz on May 30, 1943, as World War II was in high gear and concentration camps were being utilized to "liquidate" millions of people. At age 32, he had grown up Catholic but had long been a Nazi enthusiast. In school, his specialty had been physical anthropology and genetics, and he was fully committed to using science in the service of the Nazi vision. When he spotted opportunities for research at Auschwitz, he requested the position.

In charge of the "selections" process, he'd watch the incoming prisoners and decide each person's fate. He might have someone shot on the spot or sent straight to the gas chamber. Anyone who saw him had no doubt how much he enjoyed exercising his power over life and death. Among his tasks was to improve the camp's "efficiency," and he had a staff of physicians whom he instructed in giving phenol injections to quickly terminate lives. Completely unmoved by pleas for mercy, Mengele maintained a clinical distance. The people herded into camps were nothing more to him than potential subjects for his experiments.

Mengele's great passion was his research on twins. When he selected a pair of identical children who looked promising, he kept meticulous records on what he did with them. He weighed, measured, and compared them, withdrew blood, and questioned them about their family histories. Some he would kill for dissection, while others were preserved for more fiendish activities. He might operate (without anesthesia) to remove limbs or sexual organs, and even performed sex-change operations. If one twin died during these experiments, the other was gassed.

Into some children Mengele injected various substances to see what happened or how they reacted, often damaging or killing them. This did not matter to him; there were always more on the way. Even as he targeted these children for mutilation or death, he'd play with them and show an uncle's affection. They often liked him. But for him, they were only specimens. While some of his staff thought him scientifically irresponsible, he viewed this access to such a wealth of subjects, with no ethical or legal accountability, as a true scientist's dream. He embraced the ideal of the genetic cultivation of a superior race.

After the war ended and Germany lost, Mengele fled to South America to avoid capture. He died there in 1979, and his remains were identified by a team of forensic anthropologists. Yet his evil lives on in the depictions of a cruel doctor who killed without conscience.[6]

At a time when medicine was more primitive, some medical caretakers exploited the ignorance of their patients and the inability of authorities to fully investigate healthcare-related murders. Let's look at some of the nurses in history who exploited these conditions.

MORE EXPLOITATION

Nurse Jane Toppan enjoyed drugging her patients and holding them close to her as they expired so that she could experience the death process. There are few female lust killers, but she is among them. Shockingly, it was rather easy for her to move among her targeted prey.

Toppan was born in 1857 as Honora Kelley, and her father, Peter Kelley, was an abusive alcoholic. Her mother had died of consumption when Jane was just a child, and her father had turned Jane and her sister over to the Boston Female Asylum. She remained there two years, until she was eight years old, at which point Toppan was indentured to the home of Mrs. Ann C. Toppan in Lowell, Massachusetts. Taking their family name, she became Jane Toppan.

She was gregarious and had a flair for telling stories. Thus, she also had a flair for lying and for blaming others for deeds she had done herself. She was envious of her foster sister, Elizabeth, for being the heir to the Toppan household and for having clothing and goods that she was denied. Because she gained weight, Toppan had few romantic prospects to provide a better life, so in 1885, she moved out and started training to be a nurse. She acquired an enduring nickname, Jolly Jane, because patients and colleagues liked her, despite her annoying habit of lying. Little did they know.

Toppan manipulated the system, primitive as it was, with no one the wiser. For those patients she liked, she fabricated symptoms on their chart or gave them medicine to make them slightly sick, to keep them bedridden. That was harmless enough, but it was the patients Jane disliked who inspired more sinister activity. On them, she conducted experiments with morphine and atropine. Morphine caused the breathing to slow and pupils to contract, while atropine had the opposite effect and could even produce convulsions. Toppan would try various strengths and it was possible that some people died as a result.

She continued this practice as she moved on to the Massachusetts General Hospital, and there appeared to be a number of victims there. In fact, rumors arose about Toppan, including the possibility that she had falsified records, stolen items from patients and staff, and given improper dosages. She denied all charges and attempted to blame others, but eventually was forced to leave.

After Toppan was finally arrested, one of the patients at Massachusetts General described her experience with Jolly Jane. Amelia Phinney said that one night, Nurse Toppan had given her medication that had sent her into a semi-conscious stupor. Yet she was conscious enough to realize that the nurse had crawled into bed with her and was holding her. Amelia resisted the medicine being forced on her, and then a disturbance outside the room caused Nurse Toppan to leave. It's likely that Amelia had just escaped being killed.

Toppan returned to Cambridge Hospital to get her license, but she was careless and continued to swipe things and drug patients. Reported for dispensing drugs with little regard for dosage, she was dismissed, so in 1891, when she was 34, Toppan decided to become a private nurse in Cambridge. She proved to be a good one and her services were soon in demand. In fact, she carried on with this practice for some eight years and during that time, several people died.

Among them was a landlord, Israel Dunham, whom she poisoned, although the authorities decided he had died from heart failure. Eventually Toppan also poisoned his wife with what was to become her signature weapon: dissolving atropine and morphine in Hunyadi mineral water. She was not caught, and she turned her eye toward other possible victims.

Every summer, Toppan vacationed in Cataumet, on Cape Cod. In 1899, she invited her foster sister there for the summer. It's no surprise, given Toppan's longstanding resentment, that Elizabeth slipped into a coma. Toppan summoned her husband, Oramel Brigham, but Elizabeth died before he could do anything. He believed that Toppan had stolen money from Elizabeth, but she denied it. Her secret was that she had killed Elizabeth slowly, as payback for Elizabeth having a much better life. Toppan had even held her as she succumbed to the drugs.

Other patients, too, had convulsions while in Toppan's care, and many lost valuable items or even positions that Toppan sought for herself. Then she met the Davis family while renting a cabin from them. Alden and Mattie Davis owned a large estate and had two grown daughters, Minnie and Genevieve, who were both married. The Davises liked Toppan and often forgave her rent, which mounted over the years until she owed them $500. One day, Mattie went to where Jane lived in the city to collect. While dining with Toppan, she became ill. Jane summoned a doctor, who accepted her diagnosis of diabetes. Jane took care of Mattie for a week until she finally died. For Toppan, it had been great fun to have a patient completely at her mercy for that long.

The Davis family, grief-stricken, asked Toppan to help run their household. They had no idea they were bringing their killer into their midst, and soon, they were dying, one by one. Toppan gave the last survivor, Minnie, some cocoa wine in which she had dissolved morphine, and when Minnie felt ill, Toppan made her drink the special Hunyadi water. In this case, instead of holding the victim, Toppan held Minnie's 10-year-old son Jesse while his mother slowly died. That occurred on August 13, 1901 and the cause of death was listed as exhaustion.

However, there were others in this family who questioned this series of unexpected deaths of perfectly healthy people. The common factor in all of them was Jane Toppan. Minnie's father-in-law, Captain Gibbs, was among the suspicious parties. He enlisted the help of Dr. Edward S. Wood, a renowned toxicologist and professor at Harvard Medical School. Minnie's body was exhumed and toxicological tests showed high levels of arsenic in her organs. However, since arsenic was also present in the embalming fluid, they tested for other poisons. It was then that they found lethal levels of morphine and atropine.

During this time, Toppan was with Oramel Brigham, her late foster sister's widower. His sister was there as well, and she was soon dead. The same fate nearly befell Brigham, but just in time he ordered Toppan from his home. Two months later, she was under arrest for the murder of Minnie Gibbs. Several more exhumations added Genevieve Gordon and Alden Davis to the list of charges as well. Toppan pleaded not guilty.

Three respected psychiatrists examined Toppan, noting her lack of remorse when she confessed to the murders. She claimed she had had an "irresistible sexual impulse" that made her kill, because she grew overly excited in the presence of a dying person. Since she was female, the psychiatrists all decided she was mentally ill. They checked her background and determined that mental weakness ran in her family; indeed, her lack of moral sensibility had been evident since childhood. A liar and thief, she had indulged these habits wherever she went. They presumed that having an alcoholic father and being abandoned at an early age had worked on her mind. The doctors decided that Toppan could not appreciate the seriousness of her crime, so she was legally insane.

Toppan's trial was brief. The judge instructed the jury that in view of the testimony from the psychiatric experts, there was only one possible finding: not guilty by reason of insanity. That was the verdict and Toppan was sentenced to be held for the remainder of her life in a psychiatric hospital. It came out that she had named 31 separate victims but admitted there had been more, possibly over one hundred. She died in 1938 at the age of 81.[7]

CONVENIENT ARRANGEMENTS

Perhaps not as dramatic but just as exploitive of her medical abilities, another Massachusetts-based nurse, Sarah Jane Robinson, used murder during the 1880s to take care of people in her life who had become problems. When rent was overdue, for example, she poisoned her landlord, and when she tired of her husband, he died as well. So did three of their eight children and her sister, Annie.

Robinson told Annie's husband, Arthur, that before she died Annie had said she wanted him and their two children to move in with her. He apparently went along with this plan, and three weeks later, one of the children died. Robinson persuaded Arthur to make her the beneficiary of his life insurance policy, in case something happened to him. Obviously gullible, he did so. It wasn't long before Robinson reported a premonition about his death—and she was right! Since she'd had the foresight to arrange his insurance before this untimely death, she pocketed $2,000. That gave her an idea, and soon the children were insured as well. In 1886, Robinson's oldest daughter had died, and then her nephew. After she turned her energy on one of her sons, Dr. Emory White grew suspicious. He sent a sample of the boy's vomit to a toxicologist, who confirmed the presence of arsenic.

The authorities exhumed six bodies and found lethal levels of arsenic in all of them, so Robinson was arrested and went to trial for murder. Found guilty, she was initially sentenced to hang, but her sentence was later commuted to life.[8]

EASY TARGETS

Another nurse of note from history was Antoinette Scieri, who operated in France for two years, from 1924 to 1926. She provided private nursing care for the elderly, mostly men; gaining their trust and gratitude, she would then poison them for profit. A forger and thief, Scieri also served a number of stints in jail for violent episodes. When she was caught after poisoning one of her victims, she confessed to 12 murders. Convicted, she was condemned to die. The judge at her trial said that the label "monster" was not strong enough to describe her. Nevertheless, her sentence was commuted to life.[9]

While not strictly healthcare workers, the so-called baby farmers must be mentioned in this historical context, because they purported to be a type of nurse and some of them exploited the social conditions to enrich themselves and repeatedly commit murder. Their victims were among the most helpless.

There are several examples of this despicable trade, but we'll highlight a known case of team killers, Amelia Sach and Annie Walters. Sach set up a home for unwed mothers in London around 1900, aware that certain wealthy women who were unhappily pregnant, as well as mothers of unmarried daughters, would pay to have the problem eliminated so they could lead their lives without the burden or ostracism. To assuage their guilt as well as persuade prospective clients to put themselves into Sach's hands, Sach promised that the babies would be adopted into loving families. Mothers-to-be could come to her facility for the last months of their maternity confinement, give birth, and be on their way with society none the wiser. The services were entirely confidential—and expensive.

After a birth, Sach turned the infants over to the mentally challenged Walters to dispose of. Walters smothered or poisoned them and tossed their bodies into the Thames Rivers. Yet when she brought a baby back to her rented rooms one day, she undermined the operation. Her landlord was also a police officer, and she told him a convoluted story, then got rid of the child a few months later. He launched an investigation, which turned up the criminal operation and the two women were finally arrested. Since Sach had kept no records, there was no way of knowing the final tally of their small victims, but Sach and Walters had operated for a couple of years, so it was likely there had been dozens. Both were convicted of murder and fraud, and in 1903 they were executed.[10]

From the past to the present, let's examine the cases of HCSKs that might be more familiar from press reports. We'll start with the doctors.

3

The Doctors

DR. X

A story in *Time* magazine in March 1976 described a series of apparent murders in Riverdell Hospital, a small osteopathic facility in Oradell, New Jersey, not far from Manhattan. Thirteen patients had died between December 1965 and October 1966, under mysterious circumstances. While each had recently undergone routine surgery, they were all expected to fully recover and had been doing just fine. An anonymous source familiar with the hospital (which turned out to be a surgeon) passed the information to a *New York Times* reporter, Myron Farber, and he learned that another surgeon was the chief suspect. He referred to the man as "Doctor X," because an investigation had turned up insufficient evidence to charge the man with anything.

The case was reopened during the 1970s, as the county prosecutor collected circumstantial information. It seemed that Dr. X had been on duty during each of the deaths, and had been in close proximity to them. None of the victims had been his patient, but in his hospital locker investigators had found 18 vials of curare, a muscle relaxant that has the ability to paralyze the respiratory system, and many were empty. Dr. X insisted that he had been experimenting on "dying dogs." Since it was not possible to detect curare in muscle, given the time frame since the patients had died, the earliest investigation had been dropped. However, five bodies were exhumed and tissues sent for a state-of-the-art analysis. Traces of curare were found in all five, so in May 1976 a grand jury indicted the surgeon and the press identified him as Dr. Mario Jascalevich, an Argentine immigrant.

At his trial, two murder charges were dismissed early on for lack of evidence, but the rest of the proceeding lasted 34 weeks. The motive the prosecutor attributed to Jascalevich was an attempt to discredit other doctors who were challenging his position as chief surgeon, while the defense said he was being framed. The defense attorney had 21 experts who insisted that curare could not be found in muscle tissue from bodies that had been dead and buried for a decade. Thus, on October 24, the surgeon was acquitted, whereupon he returned to his native country. He died in 1984 and the Riverdell Hospital murders went unsolved.[1]

The available cases of murdering physicians indicate that doctors often kill from the desire to feel a sense of power over patients or they turn to murder to satisfy an experimental curiosity. They feel superior to their patients and other staff members, and thus their decision to kill is often narcissistic and fueled by fantasies of power and entitlement. Aside from Dr. Hazzard during the early 1900s, who was convicted of only one case of manslaughter, we have yet to document a female doctor who became an outright serial killer within a medical context. However, of those male physicians who committed repeat murder for their own satisfaction, Dr. Michael Swango is among the most notorious.

DOUBLE-O SWANGO

A former Marine, Swango entered medical school in 1980 at Southern Illinois University. It was clear to his colleagues right away that he was a wild card, both lazy and ill-mannered. He apparently had little patience with the ill, but he seemed overly fascinated with those patients who were dying. Despite a poor showing in his studies, in 1983 Swango obtained an internship at the Ohio State University Medical Center.

Among the patients he treated was Ruth Barrick. She had hit her head and nearly died, but after treatment was doing well. Swango mentioned to a nurse that he was going to check on her. The nurse thought this was strange, so she later checked on Barrick herself and found the woman barely breathing. Catching the emergency and calling a code to alert others, the nurse and medical team managed to stabilize Barrick's vital signs and she recovered.

A few days later, Swango entered Barrick's room again. Another nurse noticed him and spotted several syringes. Swango spent half an hour in the room, and the nurse once again found Barrick in a bad state. While she administered mouth-to-mouth resuscitation, she said later that she heard Dr. Swango come in and say, "That is so disgusting." Yet her efforts were useless. Ruth Barrick was dead. The nurse could not help but think that Swango had done something to cause it.

Mrs. Barrick was not the only one to die mysteriously during Swango's tenure there. Before he left for other employment, five patients had died in a similar manner and several had grown terribly ill. Even so, despite nurses' reports, their concerns were dismissed. A brief investigation was conducted, clearing Swango of any potential charges, but he nevertheless resigned.

It wasn't just the patients who were vulnerable to him either. One day, he gave a "spicy" chicken dinner to several coworkers, and they all grew ill afterward. No one knew what he might have added to the food, but those who knew him believed he had experimented on them.

Throughout his medical career, people covered for Swango. His fellow students knew that he was unfit for a medical career, and they even called him "Double-O Swango" because he seemed to have a black thumb when it came to administering medical care. People kept getting worse or dying. The "double-O" referred to James Bond, and the joke was that Swango had a license to kill.

Yet despite the concerns of those who worked closely with him, this athletic, blue-eyed blonde always managed to charm his superiors into believing him. He had a lackluster performance, but he kept sliding through the system. Few people were aware that he sometimes thought he had an evil purpose in life or that he collected articles and photos about disasters and car crashes. He also owned books on the occult and on serial killers, and among the books he'd read was one about a physician who had murdered his wife.

After leaving Ohio State University, Swango returned to Illinois and joined a team of paramedics at the Adams County Ambulance Service, and one of them later remembered how Swango had described his ultimate fantasy: Swango is called on the site of an accident in which a busload of children has been hit head-on by a tractor trailer filled with gasoline. As Swango arrives on the scene, another bus plows into the wreckage, causing a massive explosion of the gas-filled truck. The force of the explosion throws the children's bodies onto nearby barbed-wire fences. Swango "would see kids hurled into barbed-wire fences, onto the telephone poles, on the street, burning."[2] This should have been a bright red flag to people in the medical establishment. He also described how he would love to go on a cross-country killing spree and wished he'd been on the scene of the 1984 mass murder at a McDonald's restaurant in San Ysidro, California, which resulted in 21 dead. (Reportedly he said that every time he thinks of a good idea, someone beats him to it and he allegedly told a female paramedic he'd like to plunge a hatchet into the back of her head.)

But he didn't stop at fantasy, and eventually he went too far. One day Swango brought in a box of doughnuts, and four of his fellow workers who partook of it got severely ill, for no apparent reason. Another time, he offered soft drinks to two colleagues, who also got sick. They believed Swango was poisoning them, but he shrugged off their concerns, despite the poison found in his locker and home. Indeed, it was in sufficient amounts for the police to arrest him. On August 23, 1985, Swango was convicted of six counts of aggravated battery and he received a five-year sentence.

Despite this, when he got out after serving only two years, Swango was accepted into several more positions in West Virginia, South Dakota, and New York. He simply lied, faked his credentials, falsified his criminal record, used aliases, and made sure no one knew about his past history. He even forged a letter from the Governor of Virginia, stating that his civil rights were restored, based on exemplary reports from colleagues. Then whenever people got sick or died, he'd leave before authorities were able to investigate. The one snag was his attempt to join the American Medical Association. They checked his records more thoroughly than the various medical facilities had done and warned Swango's employer about his conviction for poisoning. This time, Swango was sent packing. Around this same time, his fiancée killed herself and he reacted with little emotion; in fact, he thought she should have handled her depression better than she had.

But he landed on his feet: He was able to get a job at the Northport Veteran's Administration Medical Center at the Stony Brook School of Medicine. He didn't try to practice as a doctor but instead posed as a resident in psychiatry, which gave him access to patients, some of whom died for no apparent reason. But his employer from South Dakota tracked him down and called the medical center to alert them. The dean fired Swango and alerted other schools and teaching hospitals about him.

While this might have discouraged someone less devious and arrogant, Swango simply looked to opportunities abroad, knowing that plenty of places would welcome a doctor with training in the United States. In 1994, he went to Zimbabwe, getting work at Mnene Hospital. For a year, he managed to experiment on patients until an investigation revealed him as a killer. He was arrested and charged with five murders, but fled the country before his case came to trial. He found various short-term positions in Europe and Africa. During one of his flights, he passed through Chicago, and there he was finally brought to ground. The FBI arrested him in June 1997.

It took three years, but Swango was finally tried for murder. By this time, he had served at seven different hospitals, overdosing patients with prescription medicine or using arsenic for coworkers. In many cases, someone had seen him with a syringe, and several patients who recovered indicated that it was "the blond doctor" who had injected them before they lost the ability to feel and move. The FBI estimated that he may have been responsible for directly causing well over 30 deaths. Apparently he just liked to see what would happen when he did specific things to a human being, whether patient or colleague.

Arraigned on July 17, 2000, Swango pled guilty to fatally poisoning three patients in 1993 at a New York hospital. In addition, he was convicted of another murder in Ohio. In a plea deal, he was sentenced to life in prison without the possibility of parole. How much more he might tell one day is still up in the air. The investigation continues.

In his diary, Swango said he killed for pleasure, and many colleagues recounted his fascination with serial killers, especially those who managed to deflect attention for some time so they could get away with it and keep going. He embraced the notion of killing repeatedly without accountability. He even stated in a diary that murder was his way of "reminding himself that he was alive."[3]

Despite Swango's outright abuse of patients, his numbers pale in comparison to a physician in England who was well-regarded in the community in which he practiced. Little did his patients know what he *really* thought of them.

THE MAN WHO MADE HOUSE CALLS

When Kathleen Grundy died at the age of 81 on June 24, 1998, the people in her family and community were shocked. She had not suffered ill health and was in fact a sprightly, busy woman who owned two homes and did a lot of volunteer work in her neighborhood of Gee Cross, in Hyde, England. When found that afternoon, she was curled up, fully clothed, in her home. Her doctor, Harold Frederick Shipman, was summoned and he did a cursory analysis, declaring the cause of death a heart attack, but writing "old age" on her death certificate—an uncommon notation. He had seen her that very morning, he said, and she had mentioned feeling out of sorts. He suggested this had been a precursor to her heart attack, not an uncommon symptom among the elderly.

It soon came to light that Mrs. Grundy, a widow of considerable means, had sent a will just the day before, along with a crudely written note, to a local law firm with whom she had never done business. The badly typed note indicated that she wished for Dr. Shipman to inherit the bulk of her estate. Another poorly typed note arrived four days later, from a man no one knew or could find, who affirmed that he had witnessed the will's signing. The law firm was far from satisfied with this state of affairs, and soon Mrs. Grundy's daughter, Angela Woodruff, was contacted. An attorney herself, she had always dealt with her mother's legal affairs. Despite her shock over her mother's sudden passing, she managed to alert officials to something amiss with the will. She suspected a forgery.

For one, the signature did not match her mother's. For another, her mother had been a secretary and would not have written such a clumsy letter to a law firm. In addition, her mother had loved her children and grandchildren and would not have deprived them entirely of the estate—estimated at nearly $700,000—that she and her husband had built. There had been no family squabble, no need to believe that Mrs. Grundy had suddenly changed her mind, no dementia, and no discussions with her that foreshadowed this strange behavior. In addition, to that point she had suffered no heart problems.

The circumstances under which two patients of Dr. Shipman's had supposedly witnessed the signing of the will were confused as well, with neither of them aware of what they were witnessing and both of their signatures further forged.

When Dr. Shipman's surgery was searched, the typewriter was produced on which the notes had been written, but he claimed that Mrs. Grundy had often borrowed it, so it made sense that those could still have been written by her or someone who was in her home (except that she surely could have afforded her own typewriter). Since Shipman was a respected and popular doctor in Hyde, there was little reason to question him, except that several people involved in the investigation recalled that his name had come up earlier that year, in March, as a common element in the high death toll of a number of patients in the community. He had been countersigning a lot of forms for cremations among elderly women as well. At that time, the police could not find sufficient evidence to bring charges against him.[4]

What appeared at first to be a case of forgery and fraud took on a more ominous tone: the investigators wondered if the good doctor might have actually killed Mrs. Grundy to claim her estate for himself. In the room he used as his surgery they found many items of jewelry such as elderly women might wear, which would not have fit his overweight wife, Primrose, and which made the situation even more troubling. First, had he killed Kathleen Grundy to claim her estate, and second, had he killed other patients? Had he taken trophies?

An exhumation was ordered and a month after she had died, Mrs. Grundy's body was raised from the earth. Oddly enough, her new will had requested that she be cremated, but her daughter, who had long known her wishes for a proper burial, had rejected this instruction.

It took several weeks, but on September second, the toxicology report was ready: Kathleen Grundy had died from a fatal morphine overdose. But Shipman was prepared: he said that she had been a secret drug abuser and he produced a set of notes to show his record of it. Yet a closer inspection indicated that all the entries referring to this supposed addiction had been added later. In addition, Shipman claimed to have treated Mrs. Grundy for this alleged abuse on a day when he was clearly elsewhere, shopping. His lies were telling and he was soon under arrest. But even then, no one could have guessed just how extensive his killing career had been. Even after he was convicted of 15 murders in 2000 and sent to prison for life, the investigation had only just begun. A special commission was appointed to look into past cases of suspicious deaths associated with Shipman.

Harold Frederick Shipman, it seems, began killing fairly soon after he finished medical school, as stated in the sixth and final official government inquiry on January 27, 2005, and by the time he was done 25 years later, he might have been responsible for as many as 260 deaths.

Sandra Whitehead had been a student nurse in Pontefract General Hospital in West Yorkshire, a facility where Shipman had worked as a junior house officer (an interim position between leaving medical school and becoming a doctor) and where he then received his doctor's registration in 1971. He remained for nearly three years. Whitehead had reflected back over her three months there and recalled the high death rate, so she contacted the commission. She believed her colleague, who had used prescription drugs inappropriately, had been killing patients even then.

The commission, chaired by Dame Janet Smith, re-examined 137 patient deaths: 133 for which Shipman had signed a death certificate or cremation order, and four more around whom witnesses had indicated he was present. Dame Janet found Shipman at hand in at least one-third of the cases he had certified, compared to an average of 1.6 percent for other doctors. That raised red flags, as did the fact that an unusually high percentage of the deaths had occurred between 6:00 P.M. and midnight.

It was initially believed that Shipman made house calls to the elderly (mostly women), but he actually preyed on other types of patients as well. The final inquiry confirmed that Shipman appeared to have killed at least 15 patients prior to 1975. Dame Janet was suspicious about at least 24 deaths and she said that while there will never be definitive evidence in many cases, the actual figure could be as high as 284. His preferred method was an injection of diamorphine. He was sentenced to life and in 2004, just before he turned 58, he committed suicide with a bed sheet in Wakefield prison.

Although Shipman never publicly confessed, and in fact denied the truth of the allegations, John Harkin, an inmate at Preston Prison where Shipman was temporarily housed, said that the doctor confessed to killing as many as 508 patients. An investigation found no basis for that claim's accuracy.

Shipman's childhood has been researched extensively to try to understand his behavior. Born on January 14, 1946, the second of three children, into a working class home, Fred, as he was called then, was raised by his haughty mother to believe that he was superior to other people and he became something of a momma's boy. Prissy and prim, it's no surprise that he made no close friends. As a result, he did well in school and spent his free time with his nose in books. As he entered the higher grades, others grew to respect him.

Yet when Fred was 15, he started to struggle in school. He also learned that his mother had lung cancer. This apparently shattered his feelings about himself and the safe world he'd grown to trust. It also thrust a great deal of responsibility onto his young shoulders, as he became his mother's primary caretaker for two years, and it was he who had to watch as she withered away in pain. Some researchers speculate that his control over his mother's health, including how he dispensed the morphine to ease her suffering, had an adverse effect on him, which was echoed with his elderly female patients.

After Fred turned 17, he witnessed his mother's agonizing death. Directly afterward, he went running through the streets, apparently as a way to deal with it. He then kept his grief to himself. His mother had been his best friend and now he had no one to turn to. His father was still alive but had been no great influence on him. There seemed to be little, apart from his mother, that had been influential as Fred grew up. He was not a good student and had no real clarity, aside from his mother's opinion, about why he was superior to others. Uncertain of his future direction, he decided to go into medicine, and perhaps did so because he had learned how powerful it was to control what happened to people too ill to care for themselves. However, he was not very good at this profession and it required a lot of hard work for him to get a position at Leeds University Medical School. He proved to be an unremarkable student, but he graduated and got married. It wasn't long after he entered a training program that he committed murder.

Shipman's probable first victim was Margaret Thompson, 67, who was recovering from a stroke. She died in March 1971 and records indicated that Shipman had been alone with her at the time. Three males were added to the murder list as well: Thomas Cullumbine, 54; John Brewster, 84, and James Rhodes, 71. Dame Janet Smith believed that many of the patients would have died within a few hours, so Shipman had used the opportunity to experiment on them with drugs, thereby accelerating their demise. He then made unusual entries into their medical records, which included brief comments about their deaths, as well as overly elaborate comments and items crossed out. These notations were similar to those he had made with patients that he was convicted of killing. In Dame Janet's opinion, Shipman had experimented during the evening shift when fewer medical personnel would be around.

Among four additional patient deaths for which the commission found suspicious circumstances when Shipman was a young doctor was a four-year-old girl. Susan Garfitt, a cerebral palsy patient, was at Pontefract on October 11, 1972 with pneumonia. Her mother, Ann Garfitt, remembers Dr. Shipman telling her in a soothing voice that the child was going to die and that medicating her further would only prolong her suffering. Mrs. Garfitt asked him to be kind to her child and then stepped out for a cup of tea. When she returned, a nurse told her that Susie had died. She was shocked, and in retrospect she wondered if Shipman had taken her request as an unspoken consent to euthanize her daughter. Given the circumstances, the inquiry commission decided that Shipman had likely given the child a lethal injection.

He was also getting addicted to drugs. He wrote prescriptions for Pethidine, using the names of patients when he in fact intended this drug for himself. He also used the addresses of other medical facilities on the pretense of sending large quantities out. He was caught and humiliated. He had to go through rehab and pay a fine before he was able to work again as a doctor. That's when he moved to Hyde, Greater Manchester. He managed to kill a lot of people in this close-knit community, between making house calls and founding his own clinic, before he made his fatal error of forging a will. He got away with these killings, because he was able to act like a caring physician and respectable citizen. He also knew that most of his victims' families would not question their passing. Had he left Mrs. Grundy's will alone, it's likely he could have continued without much trouble.

Even as Shipman's body awaited burial, it was learned from letters he wrote while in prison that he had mocked his victims and used derogatory codes for them, such as WOW—Whining Old Woman—and FTPBI—Failed To Put Brain In. He also viewed himself as the "star" of his trial. The citizens of Hyde were certainly shocked, because he'd managed to fool them into believing he cared about them and enjoyed being among them. Reportedly, Shipman's family believed he had been murdered in his cell and had tests done to make those determinations, but there was no evidence of this charge. (On a side note, an inmate who was later placed in the cell complained that it was haunted by Shipman's ghost.)[5]

EASING THEIR PAIN

Also in England, Dr. John Bodkin Adams forged prescriptions and administered to many elderly women. Reportedly, he was included as a beneficiary in 132 wills, and it's suspected that he assisted quite a number of his patients to die. He was arrested and charged with 21 counts of murder. Tried in 1957, he admitted that he had been of service to some of his patients, but he did not consider the use of morphine to "ease their passage" to be murder. Apparently about 40 of his female patients had died under mysterious circumstances, but Adams was acquitted. He is nevertheless believed to have repeatedly committed what the law regards as murder.[6]

It's not just physicians who dream up ways to defraud their patients; a dentist was caught doing so as well, at the expense of several lives.

MURDER FOR MONEY

It took three decades, but Dr. Glennon E. Engleman, a dentist in south St. Louis, Missouri, had figured out a way to enrich himself by killing a select number of his clients. He did it slowly, with patience, so that no one would notice, and he considered himself to be quite clever. In fact, he trusted several accomplices among women whom he had charmed into helping him, giving them some of the proceeds. His modus operandi was to pick men for these women to seduce and marry, wait for a while, and then kill the husbands for their insurance benefits. This he split with the widows. He had once indicated that it took a certain kind of person to be able to kill another human being, and apparently he was proud to be among that type.

Engleman's first arrest was in 1980 for the bombing death of Sophie Marie Barrera in south St. Louis. Barrera ran a dental lab and when Engleman failed to pay his bills, she sued him to get the money. Engleman found someone to help him rig a bomb in her car, so rather than pay up, he killed her. But then it came out that this was not his first murder.

An accomplice had an attack of conscience and told police how Engleman had persuaded her to participate in one of his schemes; she said she was aware of other murders as well. Engleman and a former dental hygienist who had married Peter J. Halm were eventually convicted of shooting Halm to death in 1976. Then in 1985, Engleman pled guilty to murdering Ronald Gusewelle, 33, in East St. Louis in 1978. He had also murdered the man's elderly parents, Arthur Gusewelle, 61, and his wife, Vernita, 55, at their farmhouse the year before. Ronald's widow had estimated his estate to be around $340,000, and she and a third man were convicted of conspiring with Engleman in these murders.

James Bullock, married to one of Engleman's ex-wives, had been shot to death in 1958, and given what investigators had unearthed about Engleman, they suspected him in this incident as well. They also believed he was involved in the death in 1963 of Eric Frey, a business partner who died in what was later ruled an accident in Franklin County. Convicted of two murders, Engleman pled guilty to three more, and some investigators sensed that besides the money, Engleman also derived some satisfaction in the planning and execution of these murders. He eventually died from diabetes.[7]

SWEET DREAMS

Similar to Dr. Linda Hazzard, the fasting therapist of the early 1900s, but with different motives, Dr. Harry Bailey, a psychiatrist, set up a private psychiatric hospital in Pennant Hills, New South Wales, Australia. It operated from 1962 until 1979, when an investigation into the number of deaths of patients there shut it down. Dr. Bailey, committed suicide in 1985 at the age of 60. Ironically, many people treated there had done so as well.

While not a documented killer, like Shipman or Swango, there is still some question as to what Bailey was doing when he was chief psychiatrist at Chelmsford Hospital. He had utilized a form of therapy that he called Deep Sleep, in which he used barbiturates to induce deep comas in patients, which could last as long as a month. Supposedly, it was a general panacea for a wealth of ills, from psychosis to obesity. He would then administer electroconvulsive therapy, often without the patient's permission.

Sometimes patients died while in the coma, having contracted pneumonia, or they had a stroke or heart attack, but 15 of the 26 documented deaths were suicides that occurred after the treatment had concluded. From among those who survived were complaints of personality changes and increased substance abuse. There were also more suicides later in life. To be fair, many came for treatment for depression, so it could simply have been that the treatment failed to work. Still, it should not have taken 17 years to figure that out.

As early as 1970, an anonymous letter (discovered to have been written by a nurse who worked at Chelmsford) brought the deaths to the attention of the authorities at the Department of Health, but they learned that a police investigation was already underway, so they allowed the treatment to continue.

A scandal erupted in 1973 when a man named Barry Hart entered the clinic to have a look around. He was not there for treatment, but he was given a glass of water and a tablet, and he apparently went into a coma. He awoke two weeks later, wondering what had happened. He was in pain and suffered from various ailments that he had not had before, such as pleurisy and hallucinations. He also learned that electroconvulsive therapy had been administered without his consent, so when he recovered, he took up the cause to expose the practice. It took years, but in the end, he was awarded monetary damages.

Other investigators and interested parties sought to shut down the treatment, but one after another failed to do so. Inspections of the hospital occurred in 1978 and 1979, but there was no official evaluation of the treatment itself. Nevertheless, in 1979, with fewer patients being referred, the hospital discontinued it. Several medical professionals criticized the treatment's essential cruelty, and over the course of a decade, investigators amassed a reported 12 volumes of information about Bailey's treatment, publicly humiliating him in the process and eliciting rumors that he had experimented to see how long he could keep a patient in a coma without killing that person. Journalists kept the scandal alive, pressuring for a full-scale investigation, but then Bailey committed suicide. He probably genuinely believed in his ideas, but his cavalier attitude toward doing with patients as he pleased, including actions that worsened their conditions and contributed to their deaths, makes him at least a good suspect in serial manslaughter. Given how long he was at it and how many people suffered, he had to have known the potential effects.[8]

While these doctors have certainly committed their share of nefarious acts against their patients, nurses far outnumber them. Let's turn to a selection of the female nurses from around the world that have become documented killers.

4

The Female Nurses

THRILL KILLER

When Kristen Gilbert was on her shift on Ward C, the acute care ward of the Veteran's Affairs Medical Center in Northampton, Massachusetts, the codes for cardiac arrest rose in unprecedented numbers (especially among patients who had no heart trouble when entering). So did deaths. In fact, over a period of 14 months, Gilbert, age 33, was present for 37 deaths and 50 percent of the medical emergencies on that ward—much higher incidences than any other nurse had experienced. In her home, she kept books on poison and assisted suicide, and in a previous year, she had called in 22 of 30 code blues on her shift. Her nickname was "Angel of Death." Finally, she was stopped.

In 1996, three nurses alerted the hospital administration that they feared there was a killer among them. Several patients had just barely been saved, and there was an inexplicable shortage of the heart stimulant epinephrine in the supplies—more than 80 doses were unaccounted for. How this could have happened without anyone noticing was less an issue at that moment than finding out who had taken them and how they had been used. Several people suspected Gilbert, who seemed to enjoy the excitement of a cardiac emergency. It wasn't too farfetched to imagine that someone with access to the right drugs might inject a patient to produce this effect. When Gilbert got wind of the suspicion, she took a sudden leave of absence.

To fully investigate this matter, the authorities ordered the exhumation of the bodies of two former male patients for a more thorough toxicology analysis. The tests on the tissues showed signs consistent with epinephrine poisoning—a substance produced naturally in the body as adrenaline and thus difficult to detect as an injected substance. But epinephrine had not been prescribed for these men. In addition, there was circumstantial evidence of a possible crime. One of those patients had died shortly after Gilbert had asked if she could leave early in the event of his death. Another patient, admitted for the flu, suffered four heart attacks. A surviving patient claimed that Gilbert had pumped something into his hand that had numbed him, indicating at least that she took liberties with drugs.

Late in 1998, Gilbert was arrested and charged with four murders and three attempted murders. The authorities also determined that she had also tried to deflect the investigation with bomb threats, which had been phoned in to the hospital, and for this, she served 15 months. Further investigation turned up evidence that she had falsified records and removed sections from EKG strips. All of this behavior supported her culpability, but more evidence would be forthcoming.

After looking at reports, Assistant U.S. Attorney William M. Welch II came up with a theory: Gilbert had been involved in an affair with James Perrault, a member of the hospital security. These codes nearly always occurred during his shift and he'd come rushing to respond. That meant Gilbert could see him in action and get some quick contact. Since at the time of the trial the affair was over, it was not difficult to get Perrault to testify. He told the grand jury that Gilbert had admitted to him one day that she had killed the patients by injection. "I did it! I did it!" he claimed she had said. "I injected those guys with a certain drug. I killed those guys." This was strong testimony.

Other witnesses offered more specific evidence. Broken containers of epinephrine were discovered in a disposal bucket after a cardiac emergency, and Gilbert had been in the room of a patient who had died, whom other nurses heard cry out, "Stop! Stop! You're killing me!" According to another nurse, Gilbert carried "epi" in her pocket, and had shown it to her one day, telling her, "When you give epi to somebody who is having a heart attack, it jump-starts their heart. But if you give it to somebody with a healthy heart, it'll send them into cardiac arrest."

On Gilbert's behalf, defense attorney David P. Hoose stated that no one had witnessed her injecting any of the deceased patients. In addition, these patients could have died from health-related reasons. To discredit Perrault, Hoose said that he was reacting to the affair being dissolved, and as for the missing epinephrine, there were several nurses with drug problems on the ward. Any of them could have stolen the drug. Gilbert, the attorney insisted, was a scapegoat.

In the end, after a trial that lasted 12 weeks, Gilbert was convicted of three counts of first-degree murder, one count of second-degree murder, and two counts of attempted murder, along with other lesser charges. Her victims ranged between the ages of 35 and 68. Although she was under federal jurisdiction, which made it a case eligible for the death penalty, Gilbert was sentenced instead to life in prison. She tried to appeal but then dropped it.

At the time of her arrest, Gilbert was the divorced mother of two sons, 7 and 10, although she had not seen them in four years. She had in fact moved out of her home to be nearer to Perrault. Her father, Richard Strickland, had testified that his daughter had been raised in a middle-class home and had been both a Brownie and Girl Scout. Her great-grandfather had died a lingering death in a veteran's hospital following World War I, and he suggested that perhaps this experience had mentally affected her.

Yet Gilbert showed no remorse as surviving relatives described the lives of their loved ones, and she had also risked critically ill patients by phoning in a series of bomb threats that forced evacuation. Welch called her a "shell of a human being." Her behavior at trial, and the allegations against her by those who knew her, indicates a narcissist who believed that only her own needs and desires counted. Others were pawns in her game, not humans with equal status and rights. When she saw that she was getting away with murder, literally, it probably gave her a feeling of power that was sufficiently intoxicating to motivate her to repeat it—especially with the payoff of seeing the man who obsessed her.[1]

People like Gilbert who kill repeatedly in the healthcare community are generally intelligent. They're aware of the various ways to kill, including those easiest to hide. When caught, they often blame the hospitals for not monitoring medications. Gilbert appears to have been seeking both thrill and attention. She relied on the overdose of a drug that would be difficult to detect and selected victims from among elderly men whose deaths might not arouse suspicion.

This situation is similar with infants and young children, who are just as vulnerable to slipping away during a sudden illness. In addition, if someone tries to inject or smother them, they are unable to report it.

EVIL OR ILL?

The new nurse seemed unusually attentive with the children on the sick ward, although she never picked up crying babies and displayed little emotion whenever they died. Within two days of coming on the job at the Children's Ward Four at England's Grantham and Kesteven Hospital in Lincolnshire,

Beverley Allitt, 23, took to her duties as a nurse with enthusiasm. Although she had a history of excessive sick leave and had repeatedly failed her nursing exams, she had been granted a temporary six-month position at the under-staffed hospital. While relieved to find employment, she reportedly simmered over being turned down at another hospital in Nottingham.

On February 21, 1991, the mother of seven-week-old Liam Taylor brought him to the hospital with congested lungs. He had a bad chest cold, bordering on pneumonia. Allitt reassured his parents that the boy was in good hands. But he was soon rushed into emergency care. He recovered and Allitt volunteered for extra duty to watch over him.

Just before midnight, Liam went into another respiratory crisis, and soon his condition worsened. One nurse saw Allitt standing next to Liam, who was quite pale. Then red blotches appeared on his face and Allitt yelled for the crash team, but the boy was already beyond help. He died from cardiac arrest, which confused the other nurses. If Liam had stopped breathing, alarms should have sounded, but they hadn't. This young boy with no history of heart disease had mysteriously succumbed to heart failure. Allitt slipped away, with no one the wiser about her part in this tragedy.

Two weeks after Liam died, the Children's Ward Four received 11-year-old Timothy Hardwick, who had suffered an epileptic fit. Allitt quickly took over his care. She was quite solicitous in attending to the boy, but a few minutes after she was alone with him, she yelled that he was in cardiac arrest. The staff rushed to Timothy and found that his heart had stopped and he was turning blue. A specialist in pediatric medicine tried to save him, but finally pronounced him dead. It was completely unexpected and the autopsy failed to turn up a cause.

Five days later, in the same bed where Liam had died, one-year-old Kayley Desmond suffered from cardiac arrest. Fortunately, the crash team revived her and she was transferred to a hospital in Nottingham. Physicians there gave her a thorough examination and they found a mysterious puncture hole under her armpit, with an air bubble under the skin; however, inexplicably there was no further investigation.

Over the next four days, three more children suffered similar symptoms, even as they appeared to be getting better. One boy nearly died from insulin shock, another had a heart attack and showed high insulin levels, and a third child was saved as well, but only when removed from the hospital and taken to Nottingham.

Then a pair of two-month-old twin girls came in. Katie and Becky Phillips had been born prematurely and seemed at first to thrive, but then they suffered from gastro-enteritis. Becky came into Ward Four on April 1, 1991, where

Allitt took over her care. Two days later, Becky appeared to be hypoglycemic and cold to the touch. Although she went home that day, during the night, she went into convulsions and soon died. The pathologists could find no clear cause of death.

To take an extra precaution with Katie, the doctor had her admitted to Grantham, and as fate would have it, the nurse on duty was Beverley Allitt. It wasn't long before she was running with the baby in her arms, shouting out, "Cardiac arrest!" Indeed, Katie had stopped breathing and was quickly succumbing to a lack of oxygen. Although she was revived, two days later it happened again. This time, her lungs collapsed and it proved difficult to encourage her to breathe again. Once she was stable, they transferred her to Nottingham, where doctors found five broken ribs.

Ironically, Katie's mother, Sue Phillips, felt so grateful to Allitt for saving her baby's life that she asked her to be Katie's godmother. Allitt accepted the honor. She acted as if she'd been a hero when in fact, thanks to her this child now had cerebral palsy, paralysis, and damage to both her sight and hearing.

Four more children succumbed to the same kinds of disorders, and Allitt was always involved, but no one at Grantham was asking questions. However, people at Nottingham's hospital were beginning to suspect that something was amiss. They started to watch the children being transferred with similar conditions and finally after the death of a 15-month-old girl, Allitt's deadly activities were revealed.

Claire Peck was asthmatic and she was taken to a treatment room to have a tube put down her throat to help her breathe. Allitt was left alone with her for a few minutes, and in that space of time, the child had a heart attack. Allitt alerted the staff, and the cycle was repeated until Claire succumbed. This finally provoked an inquiry about the high number of deaths in the children's ward in this hospital. The police exhumed Claire's body and the pathologist found traces of the drug lignocaine in her tissues, a substance used in circumstances of cardiac arrest, but not in a baby.

Alarmed, Superintendent Stuart Clifton examined the other perplexing cases and found inordinately high doses of insulin. He also learned that nurse Allitt had reported the key missing to the refrigerator that contained the insulin. He checked all records, talked with parents of the victims, and installed a security camera into Ward Four.

Detectives going over the daily nursing log found pages missing that corresponded to the time period when Paul Crampton had been in the ward. They then counted up 25 separate suspicious episodes with 13 victims, four of which were dead, and they spotted a pattern: Beverley Allitt was the only person who had been involved in every episode. They arrested her, but she denied having any part in the attacks. Then a search of her home revealed parts of the missing log.

In the meantime, the police were looking into her background. They came up with a pattern that pointed to a very serious personality disorder. Allitt was thought to have suffered from both Munchausen syndrome and Munchausen syndrome by proxy. These conditions belong to the group known as factitious disorders, which are characterized by physical or psychological symptoms that are feigned, exaggerated, or self-induced. It's not typical to find both in the same person, but the core motivation—getting attention through illness—is common to both.[2]

Dr. Marc Feldman, a psychiatrist at the University of Alabama, says that Munchausen sufferers generally present dramatic symptoms, including serious self-mutilation or injecting themselves with a toxin. Often, they return to a healthcare facility over and over. They mostly just seek attention and care, although a small percentage have a different motive: they want to baffle a physician so they can feel powerful. If the medical staff at one place suspects fakery, the patient moves on to another.[3]

British physician Richard Asher published the first account of Munchausen syndrome in 1951. He described three people who went from doctor to doctor with fake illnesses. Since these imposters often tell whopping lies, Asher named the condition after Hieronymous Karl Friedrich von Munchausen, an eighteenth-century German baron who wowed his friends with endless tales of exotic adventures, all of which he fabricated.

The most common signals to doctors include

• a textbook list of symptoms;
• a long and varied history of medical work-ups;
• numerous surgical scars;
• inconsistent lab tests;
• evidence of lying in other areas, such as a name, address, or previous physician.[4]

As dangerous as these people can be toward themselves, it's when they substitute others that this behavior becomes truly depraved. That's what Beverley Allitt eventually did.

As a child, Allitt wore bandages and casts over wounds that she would use for attention but not allow to be examined. One of four children, she seemed happy during her early childhood, but then struggled with her weight as an adolescent. From that time on, she suffered from a volatile temperament, becoming aggressive toward others and complaining of a series of physical ailments that sent her into a hospital. She had gall bladder pain, headaches, urinary infections, uncontrolled vomiting, blurred vision, minor injuries, appendicitis, back trouble, and ulcers. Allitt actually persuaded a doctor to remove a perfectly healthy appendix, and then failed to heal because she kept plucking at the surgical scar.

She became a nurse, and even as she trained to be a caretaker, she did odd things that got her noticed. When she worked in a nursing home, she was suspected of smearing feces on the walls and putting it into the refrigerator for others to find. She also missed an inordinate number of workdays for reasons of illness. Her former boyfriend said that she was aggressive, manipulative, and deceptive, and she would falsely pretend to be pregnant; she once even claimed to have been raped.

When Allitt discovered that her illnesses were not inspiring the positive attention they once had, she found another venue by abusing children, and her behavior exhibited Munchausen by syndrome by proxy. Deborah Shurman-Kauflin says that people with this disorder "receive a sense of importance and self-worth from harming a child, then 'saving' the infant by rushing the child to medical care."[5]

A psychiatrist visited Allitt in prison and he believed she had these disorders, as did a pediatric specialist who spoke with her twice. Neither could get her to confess what she had done. After a series of hearings, Allitt was charged with 4 counts of murder, 11 counts of attempted murder, and 11 counts of causing grievous bodily harm.

After numerous delays due to her so-called illnesses, she went to trial at Nottingham Crown Court, where prosecutors showed the jury how she had been present at each suspicious episode, craved attention, and displayed a cold manner while babies suffered. They also pointed out that the mysterious attacks had stopped when she was taken off the ward, and indicated the high readings of insulin and the evidence of drug injection in each victim.

Pediatrics expert Roy Meadow explained how Allitt demonstrated symptoms of both factitious syndromes and described her post-arrest behavior: When hospitalized in 1991, Allitt had tampered with the thermometer to produce readings that puzzled the nurses and doctors and she punctured her right breast to inject herself with water. In his opinion, Allitt could not be cured and was a danger to others.

After a trial that lasted nearly two months (and in which the defendant attended only 16 days due to illness), on May 23, 1993, Allitt was convicted and given 13 life sentences for murder and attempted murder. Eventually she admitted to three of the murders and six assaults.

Another nurse who acted in a similar manner in the United States was also suspected of this illness, although it didn't have the same impact as it did in England.

BABY KILLER

Few people would ever suspect that someone who enters the healing profession and swears on the nurse's oath would rather see children die than be healthy. It took a lengthy investigation and the near-destruction of a doctor's career before the truth about this malignant caregiver was discovered.

In 1982, Dr. Kathleen Holland opened a pediatrics clinic in Kerville, Texas, and hired a respected licensed vocational nurse named Genene Ann Jones. Having worked at the Bexar County Medical Center Hospital in the pediatric unit, Jones came with good experience behind her. However, not long after the clinic opened, seven different children succumbed to seizures. Dr. Holland always transferred them by ambulance for treatment at Sip Peterson Hospital, and they revived. Despite the fact that these seven cases had all occurred over a brief two-month stretch, which initiated questions from staff at the receiving hospital, Holland had no answers.

But then one child, 15-month-old Chelsea McClellan, died during a seizure episode while en route from the clinic to the hospital. She had been the first patient of the day, coming in for a routine check-up. Dr. Holland ordered two inoculations, but after Nurse Jones inserted the first needle, the child experienced disturbances with her breathing. It appeared that she was having a seizure, so her mother asked Jones to desist. Jones reportedly ignored her and administered the second injection, which made Chelsea's jerk and gasp for breath. The ambulance was called, but it was too late.

Dr. Holland was devastated, as were Chelsea's parents. Jones even cried over the small body, but Holland knew it was time to look into this matter more fully—especially after she was informed about another such incident. On the same day that Chelsea died, a boy at the clinic went into seizures and respiratory arrest. He survived but his parents told Holland that her nurse had gotten rather excited about the event.

For Chelsea, Holland ordered an autopsy, but nothing was found, so the cause of death was written off as sudden infant death syndrome, or SIDS. Jones was off the hook for the moment. But her subsequent behavior was odd. A week after the funeral, Chelsea's mother went to the Garden of Memories Cemetery to lay flowers on her daughter's grave. As she approached, she spotted Genene Jones kneeling at the foot of the grave, rocking and wailing the child's name over and over. Mrs. McClellan confronted her, but Jones only stared at her with a blank expression, then rose and walked away. Just then, McClellan noticed that she had taken a small bow from the grave and left flowers in its place.

Three weeks before this incident, Holland learned from Nurse Jones that a bottle of succinylcholine, a powerful muscle relaxant that had the power to paralyze, had turned up missing. After the child's death, Jones claimed to have found the bottle. When Holland examined it, she saw that it was nearly full but there was a needle hole in the rubber top. Alarmed at this potential evidence, she questioned her nurse and to her alarm Jones suggested they just throw the bottle away to avoid raising suspicions. Holland then discovered that the bottle had been filled with saline and another bottle had been ordered but was missing, so she quickly dismissed Jones from her employ.

The police in Kerr County found enough evidence by looking into Jones's employment elsewhere to convene a grand jury. On October 12, 1982, the grand jury listened to accounts of the seizures suffered by eight children from Holland's clinic and a description of what happened the day Chelsea McClellan had died. Her body was exhumed to examine the tissues with an expensive test that had just been developed in Sweden to detect the presence of succinylcholine. The test showed that her death appeared to have been caused by an injection of the muscle relaxant. However, it was exceedingly difficult to get real proof against the nurse. No one had seen her give that specific injection, although she was the only person who had injected *something* into the child.

In February 1983, another grand jury was convened in San Antonio to look into a stunning total of 47 suspicious deaths of children at Bexar County Medical Center Hospital. All had occurred over a period of four years and all coincided with Genene Jones's tenure there. Jones was questioned by both grand juries, and along with Holland, she was named by Chelsea's parents in a wrongful death suit. Dr. Holland was devastated. She had intended only quality care for the children and Jones had seemed to her a competent and caring nurse. Yet at the end of the hearing, the grand juries indicted Jones on two counts of murder and several charges of injury to six other children.

Jones's former colleagues on the nursing staff were not surprised. Her odd behavior had alerted more than one of them to the fact that she was not normal. In fact, at times she was aggressive and often resorted to lies to manipulate others. While she claimed that she had wanted children all her life, the two to which she had given birth she had left in the care of her adoptive mother.

With the indictment, the investigation was in full swing, including digging into Jones's background. It appeared that she worked alone and had not involved Dr. Holland in her alleged schemes. Investigators wondered if the accidental death of her 14-year-old brother when she was 16 had damaged her in some manner, since she had been close to him. Perhaps it was the fact that she had been given up for adoption or that her adoptive father had died from cancer. In addition, Jones had few social skills and was viewed as desperately needy. She had a history of lying and pretending she was ill, apparently to get attention. Sexually promiscuous, she had married young but had destroyed the marriage with deception and adultery.

While she had gone into a career as a beautician, she went into training to become a vocational nurse. After only eight months at her first job at San Antonio's Methodist Hospital, she was fired, in part because she tried to make decisions in areas where she had no authority, and in part because she made rude demands on a patient who subsequently complained. It wasn't difficult for her to find another job, but she didn't last long in that one, either. Eventually she was hired in the intensive care section of the pediatric unit of Bexar County Medical Center Hospital.

According to one story, the first child that Jones picked up there had a fatal intestinal condition, and when he died shortly thereafter, she went berserk. She brought a stool into the cubicle where the body lay and sat staring at it. Her colleagues, who treated the incident professionally, did not know what to make of Jones's overreaction.

It became clear to associates that Jones liked to feel needed and would often spend long hours on the ward. However, she skipped classes on the proper handling of drugs and made medication errors. While there were sufficient grounds for dismissal several times over, the head nurse decided that there was no need to take the matter further.

By 1981, Jones requested to be put in charge of the sickest patients, and the decision was made to allow it. That placed her close to children more likely to die, and when they did, she seemed to thrive on the excitement of an emergency. Afterward, if the child could not be revived, Jones always wanted to take the corpse to the morgue. There she would sit in a chair with the tiny corpse in her arms, rocking it.

Children were dying in this unit from problems that shouldn't have been fatal. The need for resuscitation suddenly seemed constant—but only when Jones was around. Those in the most critical condition were all under her care. One child had a seizure three days in a row, but only on her shift. Jones apparently even gave herself a grim nickname—the Death Nurse. In fact, some of the staff called her duty hours the Death Shift. One rather frightening behavior was the way she made predictions about which children were going to die—and be unerringly correct. She seemed to enjoy that. Her other means for getting noticed was to go to outpatient clinics for minor physical complaints of her own, which she did more than two dozen times in just over two years. Although she was never officially diagnosed, there was talk that she might have been suffering from a form of Munchausen syndrome by proxy.

Rumors about Jones surfaced but were squelched by administration until a baby named Jose Antonio Flores, six months old, went into cardiac arrest while in her care. He was revived, but the next day, on her shift, he went into arrest again and died from bleeding, the cause of which could not be determined. Jones allowed the brother to carry the corpse, but then grabbed it and ran down the hospital corridors. No one could figure out what her behavior meant, but subsequent testing on the corpse indicated an overdose of a drug called heparin, an anticoagulant. No one had ordered it for this child, which meant that someone had injected it.

Then two resident physicians who were treating a three-month-old boy named Albert Garza found that Genene probably gave him an overdose of heparin. When they confronted her, she got angry and left, but the child recovered, so while the incident was dropped with her, it resulted in tighter control over the staff's use of this drug. In addition, those children whose health declined were to have extra lab tests.

Rolando Santos, being treated for pneumonia, suddenly had a seizure and went into cardiac arrest, with extensive unexplained bleeding. His troubles had developed or intensified on Jones's shift. With extreme measures, he survived and was moved to another ward.

Two doctors informed the hospital administration that Jones was killing children, and one of them had found a manual in her possession about how to inject heparin subcutaneously without leaving a mark; he believed she had tried this with Rolando Santos. Although both doctors urged an investigation, nothing was done at this point, so the incidents continued.

One incident involved a child suffering from smoke inhalation from a fire. Jones predicted he would die, and he did. Tests indicated there was a lethal level of dilantin in his blood. Another child came into the pediatrics unit to recover from open-heart surgery. At first, he progressed well, but on Jones's shift, he became lethargic. Then his condition deteriorated and he soon died. In full view of others, Jones grabbed a syringe and squirted fluid over the child in the sign of a cross, then repeated this bizarre gesture on herself.

Finally, a committee was formed to look into the problem. They decided to replace the LVNs with RNs on the pediatrics unit, so Jones promptly resigned. Apparently, that took care of the problem for the hospital, as there was no subsequent investigation specific to Jones or her activities. She simply moved on.

At Jones's first trial in January 1984, the prosecutor presented her as having a hero complex: She needed to take the children to the edge of death and then bring them back so she could be acclaimed their savior. One of her former colleagues reported that she had wanted to get more sick children into the intensive care unit. She had supposedly said to this person that the children were out there; one had only to find them. Yet her actions may actually have been inspired by a more mundane motive: She liked the excitement. Since these babies could not tell anyone what had happened, she was free to create one emergency after another. On February 15, Genene Jones was convicted of the intentional murder of Chelsea McClennon and received the maximum sentence of 99 years.

Her second trial commenced later that year. The evidence was circumstantial and the pharmaceutical records had been shredded, but a statistical report was convincing: An investigator stated that children were 25% more likely to have a cardiac arrest when Jones was in charge, and 10% more likely to die. A psychiatric exam failed to support an insanity defense, so Jones was found guilty of injuring another child, Rolando Santos, by injection. For this, she received another 60 years. Although she was suspected in the deaths of many other children, it was too difficult to find evidence beyond a reasonable doubt. Jones has been up for parole at least six times and each time has been denied, but by Texas law she is eligible for release in 2017.[6]

SURROGATE VICTIMS

Another nurse who received a Munchausen diagnosis was Bobbie Sue Dudley Terrell, accused in the deaths of patients in 1984 and 1985 in a series of Florida nursing homes. One of seven children, she grew up in Illinois and became a registered nurse. She was also described by acquaintances as a religious fanatic. She got married and adopted a son, but he was soon hospitalized for a drug overdose. Terrell's husband believed she was giving the boy her own pills, prescribed for her schizophrenia. She herself was hospitalized repeatedly for a series of genuine ailments and was soon under inpatient psychiatric care.

Released, she acquired employment in a nursing home, but she often fainted and even slashed her own vagina—twice—with a pair of scissors. She was apparently despondent over her infertility. Going to Florida, she worked in several nursing homes, and 12 elderly patients died in a matter of 13 days (with five in a single night in one place), some via medications they were not prescribed. Dudley was found with a stab wound to her side, which she claimed had occurred during an assault. She actually told the police there was a serial killer at large and attempted to sue the facility for damages. Suspected in the patient deaths, she was suspended and she demanded a hearing. Then she married Ron Terrell, but was soon facing murder charges. She was indicted on four counts, based on evidence from exhumations. In 1988, she pled guilty to the reduced charges of second-degree murder and received 65 years in prison.[7]

SOLUTION TO DEMANDS

In July 2002 another Texas nurse came under the gun. A high death toll during a brief period six months earlier at Nocona General hospital alerted authorities to something wrong. Generally, the hospital records showed about five to ten deaths over a four-month period, rather than two dozen. A search through the inventory turned up 20 missing vials of mivacurium chloride, a medication that doctors used to cause temporary cessation of breathing to facilitate the insertion of a breathing tube. The nurse common to these deaths was Vickie Dawn Jackson, 36, who reportedly grew annoyed when patients seemed troublesome.

An examination of the types of patients who died showed that none had fatal illnesses, but all did demand more care than usual, for such things as dementia and diarrhea. Then a search of Jackson's home turned up a used syringe in the garbage that showed traces of the missing drug. In July, she was indicted on four counts of murder.

Prosecutors believed that she injected lethal doses of mivacurium chloride through intravenous lines to kill the patients, most of them elderly. Ten bodies were exhumed to run tests, and early in 2004, Jackson was indicted on three more counts of capital murder, one count of attempted murder, and one count of injury to a disabled person. Her suspected motive was that she simply grew tired of responding to the constant needs of these patients and might well have killed more.

Insisting on her innocence, she elected to spare her daughter the agony of testifying at a trial, so she pleaded no contest to the charges and received life in prison.[8]

THE NEED FOR DATA

Beatrice Crofts Yorker, dean of the College of Health and Human Services at California State University, Los Angeles and former director of the School of Nursing at San Francisco State University, was among the first professionals to gather the cases for analysis. At the time, she was a new tenure-track faculty member at Georgia State and had chosen an alternate route via law school for her doctoral degree as a nurse. She had seen a number of child abuse cases and believed a law degree would assist her with advocacy.

At the time, the Terri Rachels case was getting attention and Yorker sensed a good venue for research. "I thought to myself, this is not the first time that a nurse has been charged with causing codes and injecting patients in a way to have them almost die and be resuscitated. I was thinking of the Genene Jones case that I had seen on the news, so I did a LexisNexis search to write a paper. To my horror, twelve cases popped up."

As she read about each one, she realized there were two types of nurses being accused of murder. "One was garden-variety murder where they killed a husband for the insurance or abused a child and it was just a coincidence that they were a nurse. I found two such cases. But the majority involved the pattern of the clusters of suspicious deaths linked to them as care providers."

She noted that Jeff Sacks at the Center for Disease Control was studying the Terri Rachels case and had been involved with the Florida Nursing Home case. To that point, such research had been strictly an epidemiologic phenomenon, so Yorker decided to gather her own research for the healthcare industry and she published her first article in 1988 in the *American Journal of Nursing* called, "Nurses Accused of Murder." It was one of the only such articles available at the time, and she used the opportunity to not just document the HCSKs, but also to describe the witch-hunt atmosphere that surrounded them, resulting in numerous civil rights violations.

Around the same time, because of her clinical work in child psychiatry, she received several referrals for a work-up for Munchausen syndrome by proxy. "That's when I asked myself," she stated, "why would a nurse do this? By looking at the Munchausen phenomenon, where these mothers were basically creating medical critical incidents, I hypothesized that instead of a child in their care, the nurses were using a patient in their care. So I substitute the Munchausen by proxy definition, such that a person creates a medical emergency using a dependent in their care."

Since that time, Yorker notes, the Munchausen syndrome has become only one of several motives. Killing patients is not always a clear-cut Munchausen dynamic, although some nurses, including males with a hero complex, have proven to be classic Munchausen.

After Yorker's article was published, British physician and toxicologist Robert Forrest contacted her. He had written a dissertation on what he called "Caregiver associated serial killings (CASK)," including many historical murders. He had dealt with the Beverly Allitt case, so they pooled their resources, met other researchers who were beginning to notice the need for analysis on HCSKs, and continued to collect and analyze cases. As a result, as of 2006 they were able to provide the most comprehensive study to date.[9]

Another associate was Paula Lampe from the Netherlands, whose theory we'll discuss below.

INTERNATIONAL CASES

In France, a nurse confessed when caught but claimed to have motives of compassion and even wrote a book about what she had done to patients. Christine Malèvre was charged with the murder of seven people in 1997 and 1998 at a lung hospital in Mantes-la-Jolie. She said that she had wanted to help them to die, at their request, adding that she had assisted around 30 patients in this manner, but then reduced that number to two. Two others, she said, had been accidents. Her book, translated as *My Confessions,* was an attempt to bring attention to the need for euthanasia for incurable and painful diseases.

However, the families of her victims denied her claims that the patients had asked for assistance of this nature. None left notes to that effect, nor had any expressed such a desire to relatives. It seemed that Malèvre had made these decisions on her own. She was sentenced in January 2003 for six of the deaths to a prison term of 10 years, and banned from working as a nurse in France once she got out.[10]

In the Netherlands in the past decade, two female nurses were found to have killed patients. One had a history of mental illness and had worked at four different hospitals, the other said she had killed people mercifully because they were suffering.

Lucy Quirina de Berk insisted she was innocent at her five-day trial in The Hague for the deaths of 13 people, as well as five attempted murders, claiming that she loved life too much to ever kill someone. The 41-year-old nurse, a former prostitute, was charged with 18 counts of murder and attempted murder at four hospitals, and was suspected in as many as 30 cases. She was also suspected in several incidents of theft, from stealing drugs to petty thefts of money and books about serial killers. Reportedly, as a child, she had been in need of attention, and had even set her family home on fire. She had tried to kill herself as many as seven times, and her father had once nearly run her down with his car.

At work, de Berk's behavior was often dramatic and theatrical, and she was possessive of patients, although she reportedly disliked the fact that very ill patients were kept alive. Yet she expressed a certain amount of disdain for the patients as well. She neglected to attend resuscitation evaluations, and most of the patients who died were about to be discharged.

By all appearances, she was a dedicated nurse, reliable and even eager to work extra hours. De Berk's victims ranged in age from a 6-month-old infant to a 91-year-old man, and the list of the drugs and poisons she was suspected of using was extensive. She apparently varied her methods, either to experiment or to deflect an investigation looking for the same substance. De Berk had a history of depression, which belied her claim to love life, and had even once advertised her own death in the papers.

Prosecutors described her as sociopathic and accused her of killing patients over a period of four and a half years. She had lied under oath about her credentials, which she admitted, had falsified her school diploma, and had stolen copies of patient records. She was also suspected of being a drug addict. Her own brother testified against her, saying she was a good liar who was capable of killing and who had shown an unhealthy attachment to terminally ill patients. Like Genene Jones, de Berk seemed to enjoy carrying dead children and preparing corpses, and after a death she would draw a lot of attention to herself. She kept diaries about her behavior and even wondered in its pages whether she might be a sociopath. She certainly described having "secrets" and "compulsions."

In March 2003, de Burk was convicted of the murders of three elderly women and a child, and she received a sentence of life in prison. Her case is currently under appeal, and there are several people working on her behalf to clear her name.[11]

Richard D. Gill did a mathematical calculation of de Berk's cases, for example, and concluded that the chance that "an innocent nurse would experience at least as many incidents as the number Lucia actually did experience" was one in eight. He claims on a Web site devoted to her that the statistical calculations that assisted in convicting her were highly flawed. He believes that her trial was tantamount to a witch-hunt, based in tunnel vision and social panic.[12]

Former nurse Paula Lampe, who has become an expert on HCSKs, especially those in Europe, followed de Berk's trial. For her, de Berk was an example of what she called the Mother Teresa syndrome—when caregivers look to their own needs rather than those of their patient and become addicted to the feeling of being needed. Lampe likened this syndrome to the first stages of falling in love. This syndrome ranges from excessive self-sacrifice to outright aggression, all in the name of meeting one's personal need for love and attention. Those who suffer from Mother Teresa syndrome are typically loners or meticulous workers, and are reliable and competent. After saving a patient, they experience an emotional high, and some nurses then start putting patients at risk so they can achieve the adrenaline rush again. When life gets hard or boring, especially, they seek ways to invigorate it. In addition, some with pent-up anger or frustration view patients as easy targets.[13]

The other nurse, referred to in records as "Martha U," was convicted in 1996 of murder in the deaths of four elderly patients. She was also suspected in nine other deaths. The subject of Lampe's first book, *The Mother Teresa Syndrome,* Martha U had worked for 20 years in a geriatric nursing home, using insulin to overdose the patients. (Insulin kills over a long stretch of time, so it's a risky substance to use for this purpose.) In two cases, the patients apparently had angered her, one by throwing food at her. Nevertheless, she insisted that she had killed to end the patients' suffering.

An investigation revealed her alleged motive to be suspect. She had murdered patients who were not terminally ill and not even as ill as others in the same room, and had resuscitated patients who might have been left to die peacefully. She had also been heard to state that she could not abide when a patient died. Martha U was a loner but also a compulsive helper. Immediately upon her arrest, she confessed. It's unclear what her true motive had been, but she seemed to have something of a hero complex, according to those who examined the case.

Lampe researched her background and found that Martha U had suffered emotional deprivation and abandonment during childhood and was forced to take on the mothering role for her siblings. She married but her marriage was full of problems. She worked steadily for two decades, and even on days off wanted to remain on call. As she confessed, she banged her head against the wall.[14]

Other female nurses have been suspected in serial murder, but it was difficult to get evidence against them that would stick. Two cases often mentioned in the literature on this subject involved hospitals in Canada and the United States. It's worth describing them, because both cases illustrate just how difficult it can be to investigate suspected HCSKs.

UNSOLVED

At the Hospital for Sick Children in Toronto, from June 1980 until March the following year, the staff noticed a significant rise in infant deaths in the cardiac ward. Some 40 deaths had occurred, which was an increase for that facility of over 600%. Most were suspicious in nature, and unexpected.

After 20 deaths, several nurses expressed their concern and an investigation was launched, but the death toll kept rising. An autopsy on one tiny victim showed that an elevated level of digoxin, a drug for regulated heart rhythm, was present in the tissues. The baby was only 27 days old and no one would have ordered this drug for an infant. Similar deaths occurred over the next few days, so the hospital called an emergency session. Administrators suspended the cardiac ward nurses for three days to search their lockers and examine their work schedules. Then another baby died on the ward from digoxin overdose and none of these nurses was there.

Some nurses reported that one of their colleagues, "Susan N," often made odd remarks and facial expressions, and 24 of the deaths had occurred during her shift, so she was arrested and charged with four counts of murder.

Yet this action didn't stop odd things from occurring at the hospital. One nurse found propanolol capsules in her salad and another saw them in her soup. That seemed to imply that Susan N. was not the culprit. Not only that, whoever was doing this had now targeted the nurses as well. Still, Susan N's trial moved forward as scheduled. Results from examinations of 36 of the infant cases were sent to Atlanta, Georgia, to the Center for Disease Control. They noted that 18 were suspicious and others were consistent with poisoning. Sixteen more charges of murder were added because they followed the same pattern as those for which Susan N had already been accused. However, there was no solid evidence against her, and ultimately the charges were dismissed. Another nurse, also suspected, was the more likely candidate for this series, but was not investigated.

Then another baby died. Gary Murphy was six months old, and his tissues showed elevated digoxin levels. No one pursued the matter, one nurse resigned, and the final official reports left the many unsolved murders open. They remain unsolved to this day.[15]

The same is true of the spate of apparent murders that occurred at the Veteran's Administration Hospital in Ann Arbor, Michigan, during the summer of 1975. Up to 40 patients had died from an inexplicable respiratory failure. Since the hospital was a government facility, the FBI stepped in, and by August, they confirmed that eight men had definitely died from unnatural causes. Declaring that a killer was at large who was using Pavulon, a muscle relaxant derived from the paralyzing drug curare, they warned that until they identified this person, any patient was vulnerable. Although the medicine was carefully controlled, it appeared that someone was getting access to it.

The investigation continued for months, with suspicion centering on two nurses from the Philippines, Lenora P. and Filipina N. They had been on duty each time the patients in question were stricken, and both were soon charged with murder. The case went to trial and several relatives of the deceased testified that one or the other of these two nurses had been seen in the vicinity of the patients—even in their rooms—during the fatal seizures.

However, the evidence was entirely circumstantial and weak. No one had actually seen either woman administer a drug and no one could link them to the Pavulon. Neither was convicted of murder, although both nurses were convicted of conspiracy and poisoning. Yet on appeal, these convictions were set aside and a new trial ordered. This time the charges were dismissed and no one else was ever prosecuted for what had clearly been serial murder.[16]

Male nurses, too, murder patients, and some have been outright healthcare predators.

5

The Male Nurses

PLAYING DOCTOR

As mentioned in the introduction, male nurses are disproportionately represented among HCSKs. While there are many more cases of female nurses who indulge in this behavior, there is a larger *percentage* of males who do it. Male registered nurses represent 5 to 7 percent of all nurses in the United States, but this group comprises more than one-third of those nurses since 1975 who have killed patients.[1] It's also clear from the cases below that their reasons reflect more diversity, from the typical claim of mercy-killing to annoyance with patients to the desire for self-empowerment.

As a child, David Robert Diaz was frequently ill, which got him a lot of attention and kept him out of school. He managed to complete about 10 grades, but then joined the Marines. Unable to meet the rigorous demands, he walked out and was discharged as unsuited to military life. His marriage collapsed as well, so he decided to pursue his childhood dream of a medical career. He managed to get into a program for vocational nursing, although he insisted that his relatives introduce him as a doctor. What he hoped to achieve was clearly beyond his abilities or credentials, a situation that generally bodes ill for those people who appear to be an easy means to their self-enhancing ends. Diaz also viewed himself as an Egyptian mystic whose prior-life incarnation had been one of royalty.

In 1981, Diaz went through several temp jobs in hospitals in southern California, often working on the quieter graveyard shifts, and at some of these places, elderly patients unexpectedly died in greater numbers than normal, often when they were not expected to. There were approximately 30 suspicious deaths in Los Angeles County, and nearly as many in Riverside and San Bernadino Counties combined. Drug tests were performed, which produced disturbing results: remarkably high levels of lidocaine, a drug used to treat irregular heartbeats. Yet given the amount used, it was clear that someone had intended to induce cardiac arrest, so these cases were categorized as homicides.

An examination of the suspicious deaths turned up Diaz as a common factor in each hospital, which provided sufficient cause for a search warrant. In his home, the police discovered several bottles of lidocaine, as well as a syringe and some morphine. Members of families of the deceased remembered him as a nurse they saw around their loved ones. In addition, Diaz had been on duty on 10 of the shifts of a 12-day period at one hospital where a number of patients had died unexpectedly.

Diaz was not one to accept this investigation lightly; he gave reasons for all the deaths, explained why he had the drugs, and then instigated multi-million-dollar lawsuits for violating his rights and besmirching his name, but each suit was dismissed in court. Thus, the investigation into patient deaths continued. They finally decided to prosecute Diaz for the 12 deaths for which they believed they had firm evidence. The victims ranged in age from 52 to 89. On November 24, 1981, the police arrested Robert Diaz for first-degree murder. Eleven victims had been killed at Community Hospital of the Valley, in Perris, California, and the twelfth victim had been hospitalized in San Gorgonio Pass Memorial Hospital in Banning. Diaz insisted he was innocent and had never given injections for any reason but to save a life. Whenever he had predicted a patient might die, that was because the patient had deteriorated so much. All he would admit to was sometimes stepping in as a doctor when the actual doctor on a case was doing nothing. But there was evidence as well: syringes with traces of lidocaine, some of which were labeled by Diaz for specific patients who had died. Diaz went for a bench trial, allowing Judge John J. Barnard to decide his fate, and on March 29, 1984, Diaz ended up convicted on all counts and sentenced to die.

Since he refused to confess, Diaz's motives were not clarified, but given his childhood illnesses and his inability to become the important medical person he had hoped to be, he might have been killing patients to feel adequate and powerful. The prosecutor assumed it was all part of some deadly game of play-acting a doctor.[2]

This appeared to be the case with another man that same decade on the other side of the country, although perhaps with a stranger mix of motives.

THE EAGLE SCOUT

At Good Samaritan Hospital on Long Island in New York, Gerolamo Kucich saw a bearded man put something into his IV and he soon felt blackness slipping over him, so he pressed his call button before he went unconscious. That action saved his life. Once revived and able to speak, Kucich told this nurses about the incident and they linked his description to a male nurse, Richard Angelo. Kucich's nurse took a urine sample and had it analyzed. It came back testing positive for the paralyzing drugs, Pavulon and Anectine, which had not been prescribed for him. That meant that Angelo had intentionally tried to kill this man.

A search of Angelo's apartment that day turned up vials of both drugs, so he was arrested. Under interrogation, he admitted that he had murdered several patients between 1987 and 1989, when he'd been caught. Ten bodies were exhumed and the paralyzing drug was found in their systems. Angelo, 26, was soon dubbed Long Island's "Angel of Death."

Originally from Lindenhurst, New Jersey, Angelo seemed to have been a normal, even honorable, young man. In fact, he had been an Eagle Scout and a volunteer fireman. It might have been the ideals and challenges of the latter activity that influenced his hospital behavior, because he apparently had developed a hero complex: He liked the idea of saving people. Since he worked as an emergency medical technician and charge nurse, he saw plenty of opportunities, so one day he took a chance. Injecting a drug into the IV tube of a patient named John Fisher, Angelo created an emergency. The man was soon in critical condition and Angelo went to work to save him, but he had under-calculated the drug's effect. Instead of reviving, Fisher died. Angelo was convinced he could make this work, so rather than back off after his initial failure, he looked for the opportunity to try it again.

"I wanted to create a situation," he later said in a taped confession, "where I would cause the patient to have some respiratory distress or some problem, and through my intervention or suggested intervention or whatever, come out looking like I knew what I was doing. I had no confidence in myself. I felt very inadequate."[3]

At times he did succeed in saving someone, but other patients to whom he administered drugs went into arrest and died. Charged with multiple counts of second-degree murder, at his 1989 trial, Angelo claimed that at the time of each incident, he had suffered from a mental disorder that precluded him from understanding the nature of his offenses. Two psychologists testified that he suffered from dissociative identity disorder, and that an alter personality had committed the acts. Being of divided mind, he had not recognized the risks to which he'd put these patients, and before he injected them, he had moved into a dissociated state. Because he felt inadequate, he had sought to create situations that would make him feel powerful and heroic.

Countering these assertions, the state's mental health experts said that while Angelo did suffer from a personality disorder, it was not one that precluded him from appreciating whether his actions were right or wrong. The jury accepted this expert opinion and convicted Angelo of two counts of second-degree murder, one count of second-degree manslaughter, one count of criminally negligent homicide, and six counts of assault. He was sentenced to 61 years to life in prison.[4]

Even after Angelo was tried and sentenced, another male nurse decided to conduct his own experiments on patients.

THE STATISTICS WERE AGAINST HIM

Before Orville Lynn Majors, Jr., LPN, joined the nursing staff at Vermillion County Hospital in Clinton, Indiana, in 1993, only around 26 people died in the intensive care unit there per year. It was a small facility with only 56 beds. But after he arrived, a higher percentage of patients died. By 1994, the death toll had risen to 101, with 67 incidents occurring in the latter half of the year (63 of them during Majors's shifts). An examination of the records indicated that in only 22 months of his service there, 147 people had died, and a significant percentage had expired while he was working. His nursing supervisor started asking questions, and by 1995 Majors's license was suspended.

Once he was gone, the death rate returned to normal. This fact launched a 1.5 million-dollar investigation that examined 160 deaths between May 1993, when Majors arrived, and February 1995. From witness testimony and evidence, it seemed that Majors would often overstep his authority and treat patients himself. But his treatment methods were anything but effective. Investigators exhumed 15 bodies to examine tissues, finding that at least six deaths were consistent with the administration of epinephrine and potassium chloride. Most of these patients had experienced an elevated blood pressure before their hearts had stopped. An independent statistical report run on all of the suspicious deaths indicated that patients were 43 percent more likely to die at the hospital if Majors was working. It seemed that he might have had a hand in the deaths of as many as 130 patients. He'd been seen injecting patients who later had died, although his position did not authorize him to administer injections.

Despite his suspension, Majors did not bother to get rid of evidence in his home. When the police arrived to search, they found a stash of suspicious syringes and needles, along with the two drugs found in deceased patients. They also located potassium chloride in vials in the van Majors drove. In December 1997, he was arrested and charged with six counts of murder. He claimed he was innocent and was quoted on news reports stating that patients can get confused when they're taking medication.

At his trial, 79 witnesses were called, some of whom had seen Majors injecting patients. Others claimed that he was callous toward patients, saying things like, "Let them die." One witness, a former roommate, stated that Majors had said that senior citizens should be gassed. Majors attributed the high percentage of deaths during his shift to his long working hours and overtime. He had simply been tired and had exercised poor judgment. That argument didn't convince the jury. On October 17, 1999, Majors was convicted of six counts of murder, for which he received life in prison.[5]

ANOTHER "HERO"

Kevin Cobb, a 38-year-old nurse who worked in the casualty department at St. Peter's Hospital in Chertsey, Surrey, England, was convicted in May 2000 of one count of manslaughter, two counts of rape, and four counts of drugging women with intent to rape. Cobb injected patients with midazolam, a powerful sedative, which causes short-term memory loss.

It also resulted in the death of fellow nurse, Susan Annis, when Cobb slipped the drug into her cider while they were eating. He had intended to rape her after the drug took effect. Instead, Ms. Annis, who had a minor heart problem, collapsed and died. Cobb portrayed himself as a hero, claiming he tried to revive her, and was seen crying at her funeral. He might have gotten away with it, but then Janine Cuddington, a patient, complained that she lost consciousness on a hospital gurney and awoke to find herself being raped. She immediately went to the police, who did tests and found traces of midazolam in her blood. Her immediate action was a key factor, because midazolam cannot be detected after 8 hours. After the police had been notified, two more rape victims came forward. Cobb was convicted and received seven life sentences, but remains a suspect in half a dozen similar incidents.[6]

CODE BLUE

Nurse Joseph Dewey Akin, 35, who worked at Cooper Green Hospital in Birmingham, Alabama, was tried in September 1992 for killing Robert J. Price, 32, a quadriplegic, with a lethal dose of lidocaine. Investigators suspected Akin in over 100 deaths over the past decade in 20 different facilities where he worked, but the investigation encountered insurmountable hurdles. Akin had long been suspected of causing many code blue medical emergencies, both in Alabama and in hospitals around the metro Atlanta area. The number of such emergencies at a facility in Georgia was unusually high while Akin was working there, and colleagues noticed that at least four types of heart drugs were missing.

At Akin's trial, Marion Albright, Price's assigned nurse, testified that when she came back from a lunch break she saw Akin walking out of Price's room. She said she had attempted to enter it to check on her patient but Akin tried to block her.

Akin's defense lawyer suggested that the initial cardiac arrest was caused by a blocked ventilation tube and that the amount of lidocaine found in the patient's body was due to the emergency team trying to save his life. The attorney also pointed out inconsistencies in nurses' testimonies and in hospital records, as well as the fact that the hospital had originally billed the Price family for the lidocaine, indicating that it was ordered for him.

But the jury decided that the circumstances warranted a conviction. When the verdict was read, Akin put his hand to his face. Afterward, a juror said to a reporter, "Too many people all placed him at the scene of the crime, and nothing he said to explain it made sense."[7]

A similar situation occurred in Japan in 2000.

MURDER BY DRIP

On Halloween night, an 11-year-old girl came to the private Hokuryo Clinic in Sendai, north of Tokyo, complaining of a stomach ache. The doctor diagnosed appendicitis and admitted her for surgery, but in less than half an hour she suffered a breathing disorder and lost consciousness. The attending nurse, Daisuke Mori, acted surprised, but in fact he knew exactly why she had deteriorated so unexpectedly: He had mixed a muscle relaxant into her intravenous saline solution.

The doctor managed to save her, but just barely. He was aware that sometimes the wrong medicine is administered and that a survey of the country that year had found that one in six nurses admitted to making serious mistakes. He did not realize that he was working side-by-side with an outright killer.

Mori, 32, was a nurse in the 18-bed Hokuryo Clinic in Miyagi Prefecture, and administrators became suspicious when some of his patients' conditions suddenly deteriorated. After he'd begun working at the clinic, in 2000 eight patients died under circumstances that seemed puzzling. One was a child who had problems with asthma and who died while his mother went to get him a fresh change of clothing. Apparently 11 more patients' conditions declined shortly after Mori handled their intravenous drips, and the other nurses called him "Fast-change Mori." Apparently, poor record-keeping on drug supplies prevented administrators from spotting the patterns and noticing drugs missing.

Two days after the police began investigations, Mori was fired. When he attempted to leave with his belongings he also tried to take empty ampoules from the clinic, which had traces of vecuronium, the primary ingredient of muscle relaxant. In 2001, Mori was arrested and charged with the murder of Yukiko Shimoyama, 89. He was also charged with four counts of attempted murder of the 11-year-old girl, a 1-year-old girl, a 4-year-old boy, and a 45-year-old man. He was a suspect in other deaths as well.

Prosecutors say he administered a muscle relaxant to his victims through an intravenous drip, replacing a bag other nurses had prepared. Mori pleaded not guilty to the charges, but in under three minutes, he confessed. Then he recanted, but he went to trial, anyway.

Prosecutors said that Mori wanted to attract attention by bringing his victims close to death and then performing emergency resuscitation on them. They added that he disliked his working conditions. Mori insisted that the clinic invented the charges in a bid to cover up medical blunders. His lawyers claim that whatever happened to the patients was due to side effects from medication, but an eyewitness testified to having seen Mori administer the drug. On March 30, 2004, in the Sendai court, Mori was convicted of one murder and four counts of attempted murder.[8]

WORKING THE ODDS

When Charles Cullen, 43, was in court in December 2003, he voluntarily admitted that over the prior 16 years in 10 different healthcare institutions, he had taken the lives of between 30 and 40 patients. He was being merciful, he said. At the conclusion of a two-year investigation, which included Cullen's review of around 240 files, Cullen had admitted to 29 murders and 6 attempted murders. Many people believe there were more.

The first alert occurred at Somerset Medical Center in Somerville, New Jersey. On the night shift of June 15, 2003, someone ordered digoxin, a heart medication, for a patient, although it had not been prescribed and nothing in the patient's history indicated a need for it. Then it was canceled on the computer, but the drug disappeared from the stock. Around the same time, someone accessed the records of Jin Kyung Han, a 40-year-old cancer patient. The next morning she went into a cardiac seizure. When blood work was done, her doctor was surprised to find a high level of digoxin in her system. She had reacted badly to this drug before and was not supposed to get any. After an antidote was administered, Han stabilized, and the doctor ordered those in charge of her care to be more careful.

Less than two weeks later, a 68-year-old Roman Catholic priest, Reverend Florian Gall, died. After the autopsy, high levels of digoxin were found in his system as well, but since he was a heart patient, this drug was not unexpected. It was just at the wrong dose.

The hospital administration sent records and samples to the New Jersey poison control center and initiated an internal investigation. Via the computer system, they were able to see who might have taken digoxin. It didn't take long to identify a pattern. On the nights prior to both patients suddenly going into critical conditions, Charles Cullen had ordered digoxin for patients under his care. He had then canceled the orders. Yet the drug was clearly missing, as if he had taken it and not put it back. No reports from his prior employment gave them reason to be suspicious.

Over the next few months, other patients suffered from having high levels of drugs in their systems, and Steven Marcus, a toxicologist and executive director of New Jersey Poison Information and Education System, warned Somerset Medical Center that they had a poisoner on their staff. He had spotted at least four cases. Administrators continued to monitor the situation throughout the fall of 2003, though it was clear that Cullen had been the common factor. Still, it seemed too soon to accuse him.

Then two more patients suffered similar overdoses and on October 31, Cullen was finally fired. Somerset County Prosecutor Wayne Forrest initiated his own investigation, starting with Cullen's work history. He found the man to have worked at an alarming number of healthcare organizations, and from some he had been fired.

On December 12, Cullen was arrested and charged with the murder of Reverend Florian Gall and the attempted murder of Jin Kyung Han. He was suspected of injecting a lethal dose of digoxin into both patients. He surrendered to the arrest and said he did not need an attorney, as he had no intention of fighting the charges. But he had already shocked detectives a few days earlier. He had told them of his record of murder.

Then he got a lawyer, public defender Johnnie Mask, who persuaded him not to give in so easily. Mask told prosecutors from New Jersey and Pennsylvania that Cullen would offer the names of his overdose victims in exchange for taking the death penalty off the table. On behalf of families who wanted closure, they agreed to the terms.

The police were busy getting evidence together and as the story got out to the public, for some it sparked a note of horrified recognition. In 1999, Northampton County coroner Zachary Lysek had told several officials that he believed there might be an "angel of death" operating at Easton Hospital. He had examined the death circumstances of a 78-year-old patient, Ottomar Schramm, and had suspected that the man had been murdered. Schramm had succumbed to a fatal dose of digoxin, a drug he should not have been given. While Lysek could not prove where Schramm had received the medication, since Schramm had transferred to the hospital from a nursing home, he requested an internal investigation. However, it was inconclusive. By this time, Cullen had moved on to St. Luke's Hospital, in nearby Bethlehem.

Nurses who worked there with Cullen apparently suspected him of something when they found opened and discarded packages of drugs and saw Cullen emerge from the room of patients who then died. He was pressured about this behavior, so he resigned and moved on. The state hired a pathologist, Dr. Isadore Mihalakis, to make a comprehensive investigation, but in March 2003, he issued a report indicating that after reviewing 67 cases, he had no proof of criminal activity. The hospital administrators did notify the Pennsylvania Board of Nursing about Cullen's unprofessional conduct, but without proof of criminal activity, there was little anyone could do. By then, he was already at work at Somerset Medical Center, having lasted only 18 days at another institution near Allentown. (He eventually admitted his part in the death of the Easton Hospital patient, Omar Schramm, as well as patients at St. Luke's.)

Over the border from Easton in Phillipsburg, New Jersey, Helen Dean, 91, was recovering from surgery at Warren Hospital for colon cancer. That was August 1993, a decade prior to the flurry of suspicion. Her son, Larry, recalled a thin male nurse entering the room and ordering him to leave. He did so, and then returned. The nurse left the room and Larry's mother seemed angry, claiming he had stuck her with a needle. Larry was aware that she was not supposed to receive any medication that morning, so he reported the incident. No one seemed concerned, but the following day, Helen grew ill. By afternoon, her heart failed and she died. Larry was certain that whoever that nurse had been had murdered his mother. He reported this to the authorities, but an investigation turned up no evidence. Cullen agreed to take a lie detector test, but the results were inconclusive. An autopsy on Helen showed nothing, either. Cullen soon resigned and moved on, but after his arrest, he admitted that Helen Dean had been among his victims.

Cullen was on the night shift, his preferred time to work, at the Liberty Nursing Home and Rehabilitation Center in Allentown, Pennsylvania, when another incident occurred. On May 7, 1998, Francis Henry was in the hospital suffering from the repercussions of a serious car accident. Nurse Kimberly Pepe was in charge of his case, and when he died, the autopsy turned up an unauthorized dose of insulin. Pepe denied that she'd given it to him, but after an inconclusive investigation, she was fired. Pepe filed a discrimination claim with the Equal Employment Opportunity Commission, in which she pointed out that Cullen had been in the room as well, attending to another patient. In addition, he was suspected of stealing drugs.

Pepe was not reinstated, but later that year Cullen was fired for an issue related to medication delivery schedules. He went from there to Easton Hospital. Liberty did notify the Pennsylvania Department of Health about the medication error, but had no power to discipline Cullen.

Before Cullen got an attorney, he had answered questions for several hours with detectives Timothy Braun and Daniel Baldwin, admitting that he intended the deaths of the patients. He told them how easy it had been to go from one place to the next, moving on as soon as suspicions were voiced, and he blamed others for letting him get away with what he'd done. He said that some of his bosses had known what he was doing but had overlooked his errors.

Cullen claimed that he had killed patients to end their suffering, which seemed viable to some who knew him, since he'd often been around critical-care and burn-ward patients. He thought these patients were being treated as nonhumans, and that was so difficult for him to watch that he decided to end their suffering. "I couldn't stop myself," he said. "I just couldn't stop."[9]

Yet as the cases were opened and people were named, it would become clear that a number of patients had not been suffering and some were even on the mend. Once again, just because a serial killer seems sincere about wanting to help, investigators should proceed with caution: the offender is often self-serving and can be dishonest. Lying is nothing new to this person. Cullen had offered reasons for killing that did not add up, but the fact that he was having trouble in nearly every area of his life during the time he was ending the lives of patients indicates a possibility that he was taking out his frustration and sense of failure on them. Perhaps killing them restored a feeling that he was in control, an issue with which he might have struggled earlier in his life.

Cullen was the youngest of nine brothers and sisters who grew up in West Orange, New Jersey. Their father was a bus driver, their mother a homemaker. Born in 1960, Cullen lived in a working-class neighborhood, in a Roman Catholic family. His father died when he was seven months old and when he was in high school, his mother was in a fatal car accident. Two of his siblings had also died young, and he cared for one of them during the process.

In 1978, Cullen dropped out of high school and enlisted in the Navy, serving on a nuclear submarine. When he was discharged in 1984, he attended the Mountainside Hospital School of Nursing. By 1988, he had his first job as a nurse. He got married and had two daughters, but that did not last. Cullen's wife had filed for a restraining order against him, based on her fear that he might endanger her and their two children. In court papers, she indicated that he had spiked people's drinks with lighter fluid, burned his daughters' books, once forgot his daughters at a babysitter's for a week, and showed extreme cruelty to the family pets. Cullen's response was that his wife was exaggerating, but she believed he was mentally ill. He apparently racked up a number of moving violations during this time as well, and he was steadily deteriorating in other ways. On January 22, 1993, Cullen received the divorce papers, and a few weeks later he was arrested for stalking another nurse. After breaking into her home and getting caught, Cullen admitted himself into a psychiatric facility. On two occasions that same year, he was accused of domestic violence, and he also tried to kill himself—a problem that his wife claimed had dogged him much of his life.

All of this was going on when he also killed the three elderly female patients in New Jersey. Then just days after his wife sent inspectors to Cullen's apartment to examine it for fire hazards she claimed were present (but weren't), Cullen killed 90-year-old Lucy Mugavero. In June, he agreed to submit to a polygraph (and passed) to show that he had not neglected his children or abused alcohol in their presence. In July, he killed 85-year-old Mary Natoli. In August, a caseworker reported that Cullen had not addressed his alcohol addiction, so the caseworker recommended that all visits with the children be supervised. During this time, Cullen also committed the misdemeanor against the nurse. Within weeks, he killed Helen Dean. The record for this one-year period clearly shows that when things went wrong, Cullen became aggressive toward those who could not protect themselves.

In 1997, signs of a troubled mind surfaced. Cullen was taken to a hospital in New Jersey for depression. He refused to provide a blood sample and afterward filed a police report against the doctor. He ended up in serious debt to this hospital. Just over two years later, he lit coals in a bathtub, sealed off his apartment, put his dog outside, and disabled the smoke detectors, to make a suicide attempt. A neighbor smelled the smoke and alerted police. When they took Cullen in, they learned that this was not his first suicide attempt.

In 1998, he filed for bankruptcy and had a pile of debts and back payments due in child support to the tune of over $66,000. He lost his dog to the animal protection agency. Yet many colleagues recalled him as a gentle person willing to put in extra hours. He was always ready to medicate people in pain.

Cullen claimed in a later interview that he had considered quitting the profession, but he had bills to pay and continuing child support. Yet he did not mention any attempt to seek another line of work. Even his counselor thought he should stop nursing, he said, because he wasn't dealing with his depression very well. He felt he had no choice but to keep doing what he was doing.

Cullen was transferred from Somerset County jail to the Anne Klein Forensic Center in Trenton, New Jersey, where a panel of professionals examined him. He surrendered his New Jersey and Pennsylvania nursing licenses. Every hospital that had ever employed Cullen looked over its records, examined its procedures, and prepared to defend its policies.

Nurses at St. Luke's told reporters they had warned authorities about Cullen, although it's not clear from the way the story was written in the local paper just who these nurses were or what steps they actually took. Still, they supposedly indicated they had kept records, and by their count, Cullen had worked just over 20 percent of the total hours available in critical care but was present for over 56 percent of the deaths.[10]

In June 2005, several newspapers published the results of a long meeting with Cullen in which he offered advice for healthcare institutions in how to make it more difficult for people like him to do what he did. One of the ways he managed to get a hold of medications was by rifling through patients' drawers or closets, because no one closely tracked those drugs. Yet once electronic drug tracking was put into place, he simply learned how to manipulate computer records. No one noticed what he was doing until he made a mistake, because the system didn't make people who got the drugs accountable for them. In another place, he recalled, a drug storage room was never locked, so it was easy for him to pilfer them. He claimed he threw away thousands of dollars worth of pharmaceuticals, but no one seemed to notice (a claim that was never verified).

There should be protocols for accountability for staff and for drug-handling procedures, he advised. Among them would be installing surveillance cameras, the use of swipe cards and bar codes, and a daily count of lethal medications. He also said there should be a national database for updating the employment history of all healthcare workers. Institutions should pass information along to one another, Cullen advised, and hospitals should pay attention to the mental health of their employees. Poor performance such as his should be reported to the state board of nursing (although that would not necessarily stop him or others from getting employment elsewhere).[11]

Cullen went to court in Somerville, New Jersey, on March 2, 2006, and received 11 life sentences, while about 20 relatives of his victims battered him with name-calling and horrendous descriptions of the emotional aftermath of his crimes. Then on March 10, he went to Allentown, Pennsylvania, but there he made a scene. Judge William Platt had apparently made a comment to the press about Cullen that Cullen did not like, so the defendant began the proceedings by saying, "Your honor, you need to step down." The judge instructed him to be quiet, but he continued to issue his own demands, so he was muzzled: a cloth was placed over his face with a mesh hood to hold it over his mouth. He continued to chant into the buffer. At the end of the hearing, he received seven more life sentences.

He went to the New Jersey State prison in Trenton to serve his 18 consecutive life sentences. Cullen is still required to assist in other investigations, even after his sentencing, according to his plea deal, so there may yet be future revelations.[12]

Even as Cullen's case came to light, a male nurse in Britain was engaged in the same lethal activity, although for a different reason.

EROTIC ENTHRALLMENT

A British nurse apparently derived a thrill when he took the life of a patient, and he managed to inject 17 people in only four months. While 15 survived, 2 died by his hand. Benjamin Geen, 25, began his risky game of thrill and chance in December 2003, and in January he succeeded in killing David Onley, 77, and Anthony Bateman, 67. He worked as a staff nurse on the night shift in the emergency department of Horton General Hospital in Banbury, Oxfordshire. He apparently bragged to one of his colleagues that whenever he was on duty, there "was always a resusc." He joked that he was "jinxed." Like a true thrill-seeker, he experimented by using different drugs. Among them were insulin, sedatives, and muscle relaxants. It wasn't difficult for him to acquire them, since he worked in the ER, where such drugs were regularly used.

Geen was finally caught in February 2004 when he administered a drug to an alcoholic who had arrived with abdominal pain and who ended up in intensive care after an inexplicable respiratory arrest. The hospital launched an investigation into the sudden rise of such incidents, questioning 30 people and documenting numerous rumors, until administrators were able to focus on Geen as a common factor. When he was arrested as he came into work one day, he had a used syringe in his pocket and a damp spot on the jacket lining where traces of two different muscle relaxants turned up.

The hospital identified 25 cases in which there was potential for wrong-doing, but then eliminated 9. Geen was acquitted of all charges in one case, which still left 17 for trial. The prosecution team suggested that his motives were a desire to be noticed and the simple thrill he got from the excitement of resuscitating patients that he had taken to the brink of death. As investigators pieced together what he had done over a period of nine weeks, it appeared that his attacks had grown bolder.

After two months of testimony about Geen's excitement over patients' respiratory failures and statements from victims who survived, the jury found him guilty of two murders and of causing grievous bodily harm to 17 patients (a few of whom had subsequently died of other causes). The judge gave Geen two life terms and recommended that that former nurse spend 30 years in prison before being considered for parole.[13]

Right after this case, two were in progress in Europe, one of which had been in the courts for a while.

MERCY

Roger Andermatt was arrested in Switzerland for the murder of 24 patients in several different nursing homes. He was also charged with the attempted murder of three more patients, and another three deaths were classified as assisted suicides. Upon his arrest, he confessed to them all.

The murders occurred between September of 1995 and June of 2001, and they took place in nursing homes in and around Lucerne. The victims, mostly women between the ages of 66 and 95, had Alzheimer's disease, or were in need of high levels of care. Andermatt said he had decided to use whatever means he could to end their suffering. He killed nine patients with lethal doses of medication, but he smothered at least eight with a plastic bag or a cloth. With 10 more, he used a combination of these methods, but as he claimed that he had killed from motives of mercy, he added that he and his nursing team felt overburdened.

Andermatt cooperated fully with the authorities, but the judge nevertheless gave him a life sentence, with a minimum of 15 years. He was also ordered to pay 75,000 Swiss francs to the relatives of four of his victims, and full court costs.[14]

THE LIBERATOR

Stephan Letter admitted early in 2005 to killing 16 patients at the Sonthofen hospital clinic in the Bavarian Alps. He'd been arrested in July 2004 after a high death toll among elderly patients had alerted clinic staff to missing medicine and to Letter's presence during the deaths; some of the medication was found in Letter's home—an amount sufficient to kill 10 people. He said he had wanted to "liberate" the souls of people he knew were suffering.

But for investigators, a confession wasn't sufficient, as Letter could always recant (and had done so the day after his initial confession). He had also admitted under interrogation that he didn't actually know how many people he had killed; it could have been more. To prove the details of Letter's confession about mixing a muscle relaxant with the respiratory drug lysthenon to administer fatal injections, authorities exhumed 42 bodies as they considering bringing even more charges against the 26-year-old nurse. However, at least six suspected victims had already been cremated, and possibly many more.

While Letter claimed he was killing people to end their misery, prosecutors suspected otherwise. Eventually 13 more charges were added, bringing the total to 29. Initially, 6 charges were for murder and 22 for manslaughter (including one attempt), while one case was viewed as "killing on demand," at a patient's request. The charges were eventually changed to 16 counts of murder, 12 of manslaughter, and 1 of killing on demand. Letter's victims had ranged in age from 40 to 95.

Chief prosecutor Herbert Pollert cited proof from the autopsies that the fatal medication had been administered. Although the drug mixture was difficult to detect in bodies buried more than a year earlier, a sophisticated analysis helped to determine that just before a patient's death, the drugs had been administered in high doses.

Shockingly, it had not taken Letter long to start killing. He'd been hired at the clinic in January 2003 and apparently gave the first injection only a month later. He stole the drugs to inject, and the mostly elderly patients died within five minutes. However, two women in their forties were subjected to Letter's special form of "mercy" as well, and at least six patients had been in no danger of dying. One woman, 73, had even made plans for when she was to be released. A few had died soon after admission, before being fully examined. Letter was given psychological assessments to try to determine if he really believed his motives, and as his trial approached, he stood by his story.

The murder trial began in Kempten, Germany in July 2006. News sources considered Letter's acts to be the "worst killing spree in postwar German history," and an attorney for relatives of the deceased said the murders had been random and "aimless." As the proceedings opened, Letter read a statement accepting his guilt and claiming he'd only wanted to help, but he did not formally testify on his own behalf.

The prosecutor used the fact that some of the patients had not been seriously ill or dying to prove murder, and in a few cases it seemed that Letter had had little contact with them. His defense attorneys argued that he was only guilty of 13 manslaughters and 2 mercy killings, saying that these patients had lost their will to live. He also stated that Letter had been inexperienced and perhaps emotionally unstable, thinking he was doing the right thing. However, presiding judge Harry Rechner said, "None of the patients was expecting an attack on their lives." He rejected claims that Letter had no evil motive, seeing only superficial interest in the patients. The prosecutor's closing statement compared Letter's spate of killing to an assembly line.

On November 20, 2006, Stephan Letter was found guilty on 28 counts—12 murders, 15 manslaughters, and 1 mercy-killing. He was sentenced to life in prison. Judge Rechner added a rider that would deny Letter automatic parole after 15 years and said that, in any event, he must never be allowed to practice as a nurse again.[15]

Both male and female HCSKs exploit conditions, watching like true predators for their opportunities. But it's not just doctors and nurses who indulge in murder. Other medical positions, from aides to therapists to managers of healthcare facilities, have also been caught red-handed.

6

Other Types of Healthcare Killers

SISTERS

Medical thriller writer Michael Palmer's novel, *The Sisterhood,* features a group of nurses who have, they believe, a truly humane idea. They form an underground organization to help suffering patients who request to die in hospitals around the country. The "club" starts because one nurse assists a patient in this manner and sees what she believes is a need for such clandestine activity, so she recruits others who agree. "Nurses bound together in mercy," the jacket copy reads, "pledged to end human suffering."

However, within this ostensibly beneficial organization, some "mercy-killers" begin to enjoy the feeling of power they experience over controlling life and death, and they take things too far. It becomes all too easy to dispense with patients, and some who should have survived end up dead. What began as a benign act of compassion eventually becomes a source of terrible evil.[1]

The Sisterhood is a horror novel, to be sure, intended only to frighten readers within the suspended frame of fiction, but this book was actually found in the possession of some of the nurses described below. For them, apparently, it became a source of inspiration, perhaps even affirmation. And because their stories are true, the notion of such an organization is even more disturbing. While HCSKs generally operate as solitary killers, there have been instances when female caretakers did join forces. We saw this phenomenon in a series of murders in Vienna, Austria.

THE DEATH PAVILION

It was a nurse's aide who initiated a six-year killing spree at the Lainz General Hospital in Vienna. Most of the victims were elderly, many terminally ill. The murders began in 1983 and by the time officials began to investigate, the death toll stood at 49.

Waltraud Wagner, 23, had a 77-year-old patient who one day asked for help to end her suffering. Many nurses in elder care units or facilities face such requests. Wagner hesitatingly obliged, overdosing the ailing woman with morphine. Once she accomplished this without being caught, she apparently felt a surge of energy. She soon recruited accomplices from the night shift to engage in this so-called mercy-killing. Maria Gruber, 19 and a nursing school dropout, was happy to join. So was Ilene Leidolf, 21. The third recruit was a grandmother, 43-year-old Stephanija Mayer. While the initial idea was to do something beneficial, they soon found pleasure in killing patients who got on their nerves. Many were not even deathly ill; they were just annoying.

Wagner showed the others how to give lethal injections with insulin and tranquilizers, and added a mechanism of her own creation: the "water cure." This brutal method involved holding a patient's nose while forcing him or her to drink water, which then filled the lungs and caused an agonizing death. Yet it was virtually undiscoverable as murder, because many elderly patients already had a certain amount of fluid in their lungs.

At first, the aides killed sporadically, but by 1987 they had escalated and rumors spread that there was a killer on Pavilion 5. Allegedly, Wagner may have killed as many as 75 patients—her own estimate before she withdrew parts of her confession. She then said she had only killed 9, although one of her accomplices placed her victim toll closer to 200.

As they grew bolder, the nurses' aides also grew careless. Over drinks one day, they relived one of their latest cases. A doctor overheard them, and he went to the police, who launched an investigation. It took six weeks, but all four women were arrested on April 7, 1989. The doctor in charge of their ward, who had been alerted to the killings a year earlier, was suspended.

While Wagner and the others insisted on selfless motives, the jury did not agree. Ultimately, Wagner was convicted of 15 murders, 17 attempted murders, and 2 counts of assault. She received life in prison. Leidolf, too, got life for five murders, while the other two drew 15 years for manslaughter and several attempted murder charges.[2]

Criminologists state that when certain people join forces to kill, their partnership provides the momentum to continue. That was certainly the case with a nurse's aide and her nursing home supervisor back in the United States.

THE MURDER GAME

There has been little to no research on female lust killers, in part because it's an unexpected phenomenon and in part because the cases are rare. However, similar to male lust murder, the female counterpart is often driven by a paraphilia (despite the fact that some experts on sexual disorders claim that females do not develop paraphilias). There's something deviant in their sexual development that consistently triggers arousal.

Catherine May Wood was described by her former husband, Ken Wood, as flighty, overly sensitive, moody, and unpredictable. She would start something and even pursue it for months, but then drop it to do something else. He said that he could never count on her to commit and believed that she had never known unconditional love. As a result, he thought, she was both needy and insecure. She surprised him once by admitting that she wondered what it would be like to stab someone. Ken said that Cathy also seemed to show no maternal affection for their daughter. Bothered by her excessive weight, she nevertheless continued to eat junk food.

The Woods separated in 1986, but not before Ken saw the kinds of friends Cathy was keeping at the nursing home where she worked as a supervisor: the Alpine Manor in Walker, Michigan. Apparently, a clique of lesbians employed there had become party friends, Cathy among them. She told Ken that she was in love with an aide, Gwendolyn Gail Graham, but that things they did together frightened her. Graham, 22, had arrived from Texas, and she sported a tough side. Seriously injured several times, she openly displayed scars on her arms. She apparently had severe reactions to what she perceived as abandonment, which included the type of self-mutilation common to people with borderline personality disorder. Graham took up with Cathy and they became lovers, then killing partners.

Alpine Manor, with over two hundred beds, averaged about 40 deaths each year, and thus, 6 unnatural deaths, especially of total care patients who required the most attention, did not stand out. One victim had gangrene, another had Alzheimer's, and all of them had been expected to die there at some point. It was an easy situation for a predator to exploit, especially with 70 staff members covering all the shifts.

According to Wood, whose tale became the primary legal record, it was Graham who first broached the subject of murder. Under interrogation, Wood described how they had practiced sexual asphyxia to achieve greater orgasms, so she thought Graham was kidding when she suggested killing a patient. Yet the linked pain and pleasure of their sexual games had become threaded with images of cruelty against others. Just talking about murder, she said, got them both sexually excited.

They started killing patients in January 1987 and continued for three months, initially attempting to select victims whose names would be part of a spelling game. The idea occurred while working on a crossword puzzle. They knew that the Alpine Manor recorded the names of patients who had died or were discharged in a book. Just for fun, they wanted to make the first initial of six names in a row, when read down, spell *murder*.

The first victim to actually die was a woman suffering from Alzheimer's disease whom both knew would be unable to fight. Her last name began with an *m*. Placing a washcloth over the woman's nose and mouth, Graham smothered her to death. However, the "Murder Game" proved too complicated to select the right patients in a way that minimized risk and also spelled the word, so they just selected patients that seemed easy to kill without discovery.

During the weeks that followed, Graham moved on to another, and then another, leaving a washcloth in the room as her "calling card." After she failed at killing one of the male patients, she stuck to females, especially those who proved difficult to care for. In one version of the story, Graham and Wood had targeted at least 20 different people, including other aides. Their new motive, said Wood, was to have something over on each other so they would be bonded "forever." With each killing, they added one more day to that time period, so that after the fourth murder they might sign a love letter, "forever and four days." Wood said she agreed to be an accomplice because she feared losing Graham, who apparently killed to relieve personal tension.

Acting as sentry, Wood watched as Graham attempted to smother elderly women, but some struggled so hard she had to back off. Oddly enough, none registered a complaint, and in fact most of the patients liked these two caregivers. In many respects, they appeared to be generally competent at their jobs.

To relive the crimes, Graham took items off the victims, such as jewelry, personal keepsakes, and socks. She and Wood placed these souvenirs at home on a special shelf. They sometimes washed down the bodies as part of the postmortem routine, and handling their deceased victims further excited them. As they succeeded, they took more risks, which included telling colleagues what they were doing, because the confessions added to their heightened sexual drive. To their delight, their accounts were dismissed as sick jokes. Wood was known to lie and play mind games, so few associates took her seriously. Even her shelf of souvenirs from patients impressed no one.

Graham then pressured Wood to take a more active role: she would have to kill one of the patients herself. Wood wasn't ready for this, or so she later claimed. This angered Graham, who took up with another woman and returned to Texas. From there, she wrote disturbing letters about wanting to smash the faces of babies in her care at another facility. Wood swore her ex-husband to secrecy and confessed everything. Despite his promise to her, Ken felt endangered by just knowing about their activities, so he notified a therapist, and a year later, the police. Wood attempted to deflect their investigation but quickly caved and blamed Graham.

After an investigation that involved two exhumations, which offered no physical evidence, both women were arrested. Wood turned state's witness against her former lover for a sentence of 20 to 40 years, with the possibility of parole. Graham, too, testified, but the most telling witness was Graham's current lover, who admitted that Graham had confessed six murders to her.

On September 20, 1989, the jury deliberated for only six hours before they rendered a verdict: Graham was convicted of five counts of first-degree murder and one count of conspiracy to commit murder. She drew six life sentences, with no possibility of parole. In media accounts, Wood's role was downplayed to "occasional lookout," and the case remains controversial today over whether there were more murders, as well as whether there were any murders at all. There is some speculation, especially after a psychological evaluation of Graham, that even if Graham did the killing, Wood had been the mastermind. However, reports about her behavior are inconsistent.[3]

These women played a game and used patients for their own gratification, but some HCSKs simply want to be rid of their patients. That, too, can become a game, and apparently did for a Midwestern man who also worked as a nurse's aide.

EVIL ASPIRATIONS

He read about serial killers and dabbled in the occult. Entering the medical profession was probably not motivated by a desire to heal or nurture. By the time he was 18, Donald Harvey was employed as an orderly. For about nine months, starting in May 1970, he worked at Marymount Hospital in London, Kentucky. According to what he later admitted, he noticed people who seemed to be suffering, so he decided to do something about it. The first patient he killed he smothered with a pillow. He also found it useful as he went along to utilize a near-empty oxygen tank to deprive them of air. He seemed to have no trouble watching them die by his hand, and over the course of his stint at this hospital, he killed at least a dozen people. During a taped interview, Harvey methodically described in chilling detachment exactly how he killed. At times, he also used injections, placing the needle where he figured no one would look.

Then Harvey was arrested, but ironically, the charge was burglary and he was fined. But he decided to move on, joining the Air Force. After a year, he was discharged and soon he was committed to a hospital himself and placed in restraints. He received numerous electroshock treatments. When he was discharged, he decided to return to hospital work, but he wanted to change his position. He became a nurse's aide at Cardinal Hill Hospital in Lexington, Kentucky, as well as working part-time at Good Samaritan. Then he moved on to the Cincinnati VA Medical Center in Ohio. This job he held onto for nearly 10 years, working variously as a nursing assistant, housekeeper and diener (autopsy assistant). (One of his former lovers had been a mortuary assistant who allegedly enjoyed having sex after hours with corpses.)

While at these facilities, Harvey stole tissue samples and took them home. Some sources indicate that he might have practiced black magic rituals that called for human flesh. He was also continuing with his so-called service to patients, killing about 15 but adding poison to his arsenal of death methods. He joked about it at times.

In 1985, Harvey was caught with a pistol in the hospital and forced to resign. At the time, he was reading a paperback biography of another serial killer, Charles Sobhraj, possibly to get ideas. Dubbed "the Serpent," Sobhraj was known as Southeast Asia's most notorious killer. A petty thief, con-man, and forger, he soon turned to murder to get money. He would drug and rob wealthy tourists, as well as his competitors in the drug trade. He also stole identities and proved difficult to capture, as he slipped from one country to another. Finally caught and convicted in Nepal for a double homicide, he was suspected in at least 20 murders across Europe and Asia.

Harvey received employment as a nurse's aide in Drake Memorial Hospital. There he killed at least 23 more patients by injecting them with different lethal substances like arsenic, cyanide, and petroleum-based cleansers. Some victims were apparently chosen by occult means, as Harvey chanted over fingernails or hair that he placed on a homemade altar. He also poisoned a few people outside the hospital. An argument with a neighbor inspired him to lace her drink with a toxic concoction and she nearly died. He poisoned a lover, whom he then nursed back to health, but whose parents weren't so lucky. The man's mother died by Harvey's hand and her husband became critically ill.

The sudden death of a patient named John Powell finally stopped Harvey in April 1987. During his autopsy, the physician detected high levels of cyanide, and he turned it over to the authorities; the death was ruled a homicide. Harvey was arrested and he told his public defender, William Whalen, that he had lost count of how many people he'd killed (including people outside the hospital), but it had not been more then 70. On Whalen's advice, Harvey pleaded not guilty by reason of insanity. Then he confessed to killing 33 people. He soon changed that number to 52, and then more than 80. He insisted that most had been mercy killings.

A psychiatrist who examined Harvey said that not only was he was legally sane, he had compulsively killed to relieve tension. He was also competent to stand trial. Instead, he elected to forgo the trial and plead guilty. On August 18, 1987, in a Cincinnati courtroom, Donald Harvey admitted to 24 counts of murder and 4 counts of attempted murder. Then he added another murder plea, all of which got him a huge fine and four consecutive life sentences. He then faced charges in Kentucky, where he entered a guilty plea on 9 of the 12 murders to which he had confessed. There he got eight life terms, plus 20 years.

Yet he wasn't finished. Returned to Cincinnati, he confessed to three more killings and three attempted murders. When he was done, he had admitted his guilt in 36 murders and 1 case of manslaughter, which gave him the U.S. record to date for HCSKs.

Harvey's defense attorney, William Whalen wrote a book, *Defending Donald Harvey,* about his experience with Harvey, to provide Harvey with the chance to tell his story and to explain himself. Harvey continued to insist that he was a mercy-killer, but the facts indicate otherwise. Over the course of 18 years in several different institutions, he killed for a number of petty reasons. One patient he simply did not like; another he killed out of revenge. And then there were the "annoying" acquaintances he poisoned with arsenic. There seems little doubt, given the evidence unearthed at his home, that Harvey was engaged in occult practices when he chose some of his victims, and the opening scene of Whalen's book even has him lighting candles that stand for specific people and deciding from a candle's flicker that the person symbolized by that candle should die. He supposedly believed he was receiving commands from some spirit named Duncan, but that might have been part of his feigned attempt at insanity. Even so, Whalen accepts the idea that Harvey's acts were somehow the result of projecting his own depression onto his patients.[4]

As if to mitigate his crimes, Harvey offered what he called help, by describing his methods and telling hospitals what they did wrong in creating situations that allowed him to kill unhampered. In other words, he continued to revel in his acts, blame others, and deflect responsibility from himself. Like many HCSKs, Harvey believes that healthcare institutions must accept a large part of the culpability. His lack of insight into his own actions is shared by the next killer, a healthcare worker in Florida with a compulsion to confess and recant.

ON A MISSION

In a nursing home in Putnam County, Florida, a male nurse's aide was arrested for his involvement in the suspicious deaths of several patients. In July 1988, a news reporter had received an anonymous tip that someone was killing patients at the New Life Acres Nursing Home, which he passed on to the sheriff's office at once. Apparently the tipster had overheard a staff member in a bar bragging about having killed five patients. Then a crisis worker called with a similar report, only this message concerned a call from the actual killer, Jeff, who had stated he'd just tried to kill someone else.

Jeff was clever, too. Instead of acting as if he belonged in a patient's room, he stated that he had entered through a cut screen so no one would see him with the person slated to die. After his sixth incident, he had decided he had a killing compulsion and he was looking for help. He offered the names of the deceased patients.

It wasn't difficult to identify the staff member as Jeffrey Lynn Feltner, 26, a nurse's aide. It turned out he was a reliable and capable employee, who worked the late shift. When investigators asked about the names that Jeff had given, it turned out they had all died between February 7 and April 6 that year. Each death had been attributed to natural causes. Two bodies had been cremated, but the three that were buried were available for exhumation.

The detectives visited Feltner and taped his denials about making the calls, but the report identified his voice on tape as the anonymous caller. Feltner was arrested, whereupon he admitted making the calls but denied that the claims he had made were true. He said he'd simply wanted to inspire an investigation of the poor nursing home conditions. In fact, in the room of the supposed murder attempt, no screen was damaged, although a chair stood outside it. Yet no one had put weight on it.

There was no evidence whatsoever that the patient deaths had been anything but natural, so the detectives assumed Feltner had been looking for attention. They certainly could not bring charges that they could make stick.

But the case did not end there. Apparently the following summer, Feltner confessed to two more murders, one at Bowman's Care in another Florida town, Ormond, and one at Clyatt Memorial Geriatric Center in Daytona Beach. This third facility gave a fair report on him, although when he'd failed to show up two days in a row, he'd been fired.

Under questioning, Feltner denied killing anyone and provided the same motive for making the confessions. The investigating detective suggested to Feltner that he check himself into a local mental health facility, which he did. But then a security guard found a list in his possession of the names of the seven dead patients, with the dates of their deaths. When confronted, Feltner confessed to killing all seven by suffocation during their sleep. His stated motive was to relieve their suffering and his method was to hold their noses and mouths while he straddled them to prevent them from struggling. It usually took about six minutes. Killing them, he said, was the only way he could see to help them.

Feltner talked about how much easier it was to get a job in a nursing home than even a fast food restaurant. So he'd continued to look for work in such places. Placed under arrest, Feltner was indicted in Daytona Beach for first-degree murder of the one patient in that county, Doris Moriarty, 88. In Putnam County, the body of Sarah Abrams, 75, was exhumed. The autopsy showed that she had died from asphyxiation.

Before his trial, Feltner slashed his wrists, but it turned out to have been a feigned attempt at suicide. Then he went on a hunger strike and would not get out of bed. He recanted his confessions, but his attorney worked out a plea deal in which he would confess to the murder of Sarah Abrams in exchange for no death penalty. He did the same for the murder of Doris Moriarty, with a reduced charge of second-degree murder. Receiving life in prison, he was not charged with the remaining five killings.[5]

KILLING FOR CURIOSITY

In 1981, Norway was faced with a serial killer when the manager of Orkdal Valley Nursing Home confessed to his crimes. Arnfinn Nesset, 46, said that he had killed 27 patients under his care. But he had also worked elsewhere, and since Nesset could not remember how many he may have killed, officials built a list of 62 possible victims. Nesset had used the paralyzing drug, curacit (from curare) to immobilize them. He claimed that some were mercy killings but also admitted to exercising morbid curiosity (and had embezzled some money). Then he recanted his confession, which meant that there was little evidence for court. Prosecutors went ahead and charged him with 25 murders, along with other crimes such as forgery and theft. He was convicted in 22 murders and given a sentence of 21 years, the maximum term possible. In 2004, Nesset was released, whereupon he reportedly went to work for the Salvation Army.[6]

OVERLOAD

Hospitals are supposed to be places of healing, but they can also attract people seeking power. It's not clear when the suspicious deaths actually began at the Glendale Adventist Medical Center in southern California, because elderly people die every day from natural causes. If they're poor or have few relatives around to remark on it, they can die without anyone noticing that perhaps they shouldn't have. However, near the end of 1996, the respiratory failure of a patient did get attention.

Salbi Asatryan, 75, was an Armenian immigrant. She was taken to the hospital on December 27 for extreme difficulty with breathing. Placed in critical care, she continued to struggle as her daughter waited, and finally she stabilized. Several respiratory therapists worked with her and believed she would pull through. It was not long before she was breathing on her own and feeding herself. But three days later, she was discovered dead in her bed.

Rumors spread around the hospital about a certain person on the night shift and his "magic syringe." Efren Saldivar, one of the respiratory therapists, had suggested that he knew how to take care of patients. Apparently he had become a therapist because he had seen a friend wearing the uniform and liked it. His friend was enrolled in the College of Medical and Dental Careers in North Hollywood, and while Saldivar had no medical aspirations, this kind of employment seemed preferable to his current job at a grocery store. In 1988, he enrolled in the technical school himself, receiving his certification at the age of 19. He also got his uniform. Reportedly, he wanted to work the night shift, because there would be less people around. Uninterested in the profession as a calling, he viewed himself as a technician.

Part of his job was to put needles into arteries, because he had to determine if patients were having difficulty breathing and if there was enough oxygen in their blood. He also managed respiratory rehabilitation and putting tubes down patients' throats when they couldn't breathe well on their own, especially during a code blue emergency, and he placed people on ventilators that had to be monitored and adjusted. He knew a lot about drugs and computers.

Saldivar developed a knack for the work, seeming to enjoy talking with patients as they waited for a medication to take effect. Eventually he went on the graveyard shift at night, working without supervision as only one of two respiratory technicians in the hospital. Yet, they might work for hours on the same shift and not encounter each other. The work wasn't difficult, emergencies were few, and Saldivar was even able to offer his services part-time to other area facilities. To those with whom he worked, he seemed a competent guy always willing to do a favor. It was difficult to see how his perspective was becoming warped. For a while he took Zoloft to ease a longstanding depression, but then stopped.

The trouble apparently arose when patients would awaken at night and request attention—even demanding it. A few were lonely, but some were chronic complainers, insisting on treatment any time, day or night. One of these was a woman named Jean C. On February 26, 1997, she pressed her button and Saldivar responded. As Jean recalled, she blacked out. She did not give the incident another thought until she heard later about the investigation.

In April, one of the other respiratory technicians suggested to his boss that Saldivar was injecting something into patients. At that time, John Bechthold was head of the department and he needed more than innuendo, so he told another supervisor what he had heard and together they increased their vigilance.

While the records showed little, Saldivar's colleagues were disturbed by certain things he said. He would talk about patients who "needed to die," and then that person died—sometimes several in a single night. Occasionally, the other respiratory technicians joked that Efren had the magic touch. But eventually he got careless.

As a practical joke, a couple of the other respiratory technicians decided to put someone else's clothing in Saldivar's locker, so on his night off, they pried it open. Someone noticed a bag and decided to open it. The bag proved to contain some very potent drugs, including morphine, the diaphragm-paralyzing drug succinylcholine chloride, and Pavulon, used to stop the breathing rhythms of patients going onto a respirator. On a shelf inside the locker were some empty syringes. No respiratory technician was allowed to handle these drugs, which were administered by physicians, so for the first time there was real evidence to support the rumors. However, they had discovered it by invading Saldivar's privacy, so they said nothing more.

Then one of the respiratory technicians, Ursula Anderson, mentioned her suspicion about Saldivar's activities to a man in a bar. As he listened, he saw an opportunity to make a few dollars, so in February of 1998, he called Glendale Adventist Medical Center. He didn't even have a name to offer in this tip, but when they went down the list of almost 40 therapists who worked there, he thought Saldivar's name sounded familiar. He didn't make any money, but the hospital now had an unrelated source telling them about the same respiratory technician reported earlier. This time, the administrators called in the Glendale Police Department and conducted their own investigation. During that time, two more respiratory unit patients died.

Sergeant John McKillop met with the administrators and they told him about both tips. There were several dead ends and the people questioned denied everything, but that did not stop the investigation. They contacted the initial tipster to find out if he knew anything more and he described the locker incident.

The detectives decided to approach Saldivar himself to see what he might say. If he was a killer, they hoped for a reaction. Saldivar was introduced to a polygraph examiner, who asked if he understood why he had been asked to come in. He responded that he expected to get his name cleared. He had heard that some anonymous caller had fingered him as a killer.

During this conversation, Saldivar initially denied doing anything to patients, but then admitted that ever since he had started working at the hospital, he'd been injecting people. His first case had happened when he was 19, fresh out of school.

He had been assigned an elderly female cancer patient on a life-support system, so far gone her family members had taken their leave. After everyone was gone, Saldivar looked in on the woman and saw that she was still breathing. He felt sorry for her. Out of mercy, he claimed, he connected two tubes, suffocating her. He did not kill again for some time after that, but a few years later, he had found a discarded bottle of Pavulon and had injected some of it through a patient's IV tube.

Although the detectives told Saldivar he had the right to remain silent and get an attorney, he waived this and talked for two hours. He said that his first lethal injection, which he stated he had done only twice, had occurred in 1997. When one detective said that he would look into that claim, Saldivar said that he'd had accomplices. They would sometimes go from room to room injecting people who shouldn't have to live any longer. Their sole motive had been mercy.

Asked if this involved more than 500 patients, Saldivar estimated it was between 40 and 50. He had been convinced they were "ready to die." Saldivar's apparent criteria for justification was that a patient had a "do not resuscitate" order, was unconscious, and was "ready." Despite his assurance that his methods had been pain-free, in fact death by Pavulon is difficult. Derived from an African drug, curare, the patient goes into a conscious paralysis and feels every minute of the death-by-suffocation process. It is no easy experience and they can't even scream for someone's attention. Their throat closes up and they have to lie there helpless until their ordeal is over.

The police went to work to corroborate the confession, in case Saldivar recanted, but they knew that the drugs he had used were difficult to detect in human tissue. They would have to find some in his possession. As Saldivar was placed under arrest, the police searched his home and found pornography but no incriminating drugs. To their frustration, after two days they had to release him. They realized that if he had a change of heart, he might destroy evidence, wherever it was. He'd been fired, so he had plenty of time on his hands. The hospital had suspended 37 other employees in the respiratory department as well.

As suspected, Saldivar soon recanted his confession. He'd had a mental disorder along with depression, he said, and the police had pressured him to confess, so he had made up a story. This new turn of events meant that physical evidence was even more important to obtain. They sorted through numerous records, learning that over 1,000 patients had died at some point on Saldivar's shift during the eight years he had worked at the hospital. They narrowed down the list to recent cases, specifically those deaths that appeared to be mysterious, and in which the body was still available. It took them a year to settle on the top 20 prospects for exhumation.

Throughout the summer months of 1999, the investigators brought potential victims out of the ground. The pathologists examined them and took tissue samples from the livers, bladders, and muscles. At first the toxicology analysis showed only negative results, but after the 20 exhumations were complete, six bodies yielded positive results. All had been elderly and one was a mentally retarded woman.

In January 2001, Saldivar, now 31, was arrested and charged with six counts of murder. Once again, he began to talk. This time he said that he'd been understaffed on some shifts, so to ease the workload he had eliminated patients. When he felt overwhelmed, he would look at the names on the board and decide who to kill.

He was imprisoned to await a trial and investigators looked into his background. Saldivar was born in Brownsville, Texas, on September 30, 1969. His mother, who lived in Mexico, went into Texas to give birth, exploiting the lack of checks in the medical system to her benefit, so her children could be U.S. citizens. His father, Alfredo, then moved his wife and two sons to Los Angeles and became a handyman. Efren's mother was a Jehovah's Witness and she raised her children in this faith. As a child, Efren applied himself in school but worked below his abilities. Teachers liked him because he had an extroverted personality, but he had a difficult time fitting in with other children. At 170 pounds, he was large and awkward, and girls he liked rejected him, which hurt his feelings. He remained withdrawn and stayed close to his family.

Saldivar admitted that he had killed patients at other hospitals where he had worked part-time. After 60 victims, he said at one point, he had lost count. He figured it was over 100. It had just been a gradual thing, an act that had bothered him a little at first but then he'd grown used to it. The idea of killing was never a plan for him and he didn't think much about it after it was accomplished.

The prosecutor prepared a case, finding a star witness in Jean C., the complaining patient whom Saldivar had attempted and failed to kill—giving him yet another charge. Ursula Anderson, the female respiratory technician who knew what Saldivar was doing, got immunity in exchange for her agreement to testify that she had given Saldivar the Pavulon and knew what he was doing with it.

Three years after the murders first came to light, the Glendale Adventist Medical Center gave a statement in a press conference. They apologized to the families and assured them that they were helping the police with the investigation. They were disheartened by the way someone would so shockingly abuse a position of trust. The hospital spokesperson said that administrators were unaware of how Saldivar obtained the drugs that he used, but as a result of this case they had tightened their controls and revised their procedures.[7]

In March 2002, Saldivar pled guilty to six counts of murder in exchange for life imprisonment rather than the death penalty. He contested nothing about the investigation and accepted his sentence, which was formally meted out on April 17. Judge Lance Ito gave Saldivar six consecutive life sentences and 15 more years for the attempted murder. Saldivar offered an apology to the families and asked for their forgiveness.[8]

While many HCSKs work in formalized healthcare systems, some work outside such hierarchies, finding ways to kill freely and repeatedly without much accountability.

WISE WOMEN

Midwives often act as shamans in small villages, and their power as healers gives them a certain status. Women in need, whether for assistance with childbirth or illness, look to the midwives. In one village in Hungary, the medicine women placed their skills in the service of multiple murder.

Nagyrev was a farming village on the River Tisza in Hungary, about 60 miles southeast of Budapest, near another town called Tiszakurt. Since there was no hospital in Nagyrev, the prominent midwife, Mrs. Julius Fuzekos (other sources indicate Fazekas), took care of people's medical needs. She had been a resident of the town for three years, since 1911, but in that time she had assisted women to have abortions. Her cohort in crime, reputed to be a witch, was Susanna Olah, a.k.a., Auntie Susi.

In 1914, most of the village's men had gone to war, but around the same time, a P.O.W. camp opened up outside town. Oddly, the Allied prisoners were allowed certain privileges, including visiting town, where they got involved with lonely housewives. As the war ended and husbands returned, some of the women were not keen about that, and sought ways to dispatch them.

Fuzekos and Olah sold "remedies" from boiling arsenic off strips of flypaper. The first death was Peter Hegedus in 1914, but it's estimated that anywhere between 5 and 50 poisoners went into action, calling themselves "The Angel Makers of Nagyrev." Due to the high death rate, the area was soon dubbed "the Murder District."

A few women appreciated how easy it was to be rid of their burdens, without much accountability, and some poisoned other annoying relatives—even children. Marie Kardos murdered her husband, her lover, and her 23-year-old son, while Maria Varga killed seven members of her family.

By some accounts, the poisonings stopped in 1929 only after a medical student from another town found high levels of arsenic in a body washed up on the riverbanks. Another account indicates that an intended victim survived a poisoning and turned the women in to authorities. In either case, officials exhumed several bodies in the Nagyrev cemetery, and finding poison, arrested 38 suspects, with more arrests to follow.

Twenty-six women actually went to trial on various charges, mostly murder. Seven received the death sentence and the others spent varying periods of time in jail. Among those who died was Auntie Susi, because it was she who had gone about town distributing the poison. One account says that Fuzekos was among those hanged, but another describes her suicide by poison in her own home, surrounded by pots of boiled flypaper, just as the police came to arrest her. At any rate, the woman who had offered so-called medical services had inspired a shocking murder spree, and the final tally will never be known.[9]

BAD MEDICINE

Ahmad Suradji, 45, was an Indonesian shaman, or sorcerer, who was locally respected for his supposed supernatural power to heal and ability to grant wishes. In 1997, he was linked with several missing women, and an investigation turned up 26 skeletons on his sugar cane plantation. Police believed these were the remains of victims, mostly prostitutes hoping to be made more beautiful. Suradji manipulated their gullibility and took their lives. The police arrested him and one of his three wives, Tumimi, who was charged as his accomplice.

Suradji readily confessed to multiple murder, saying that although he had managed to kill 42 women, his goal had been 72. In 1986, his late father had instructed him in a dream to kill this many women to fulfill a black magic ritual that would improve his shamanic skills. His victims ranged in age from 11 to 30, and the ritual called for them to be strangled with a cable after being buried up to their waists. After strangling each woman, he drank her saliva and then buried her with her head facing his home. On April 28, 1998, a judge found Suradji guilty of the murders and ordered him put to death. His wife was sentenced to death as well, by firing squad. They have been executed.[10]

7

Healthcare Practitioners Who Kill Outside the Profession

CRAZY OVER CARDS

Although numerous people who work in healthcare have murdered someone in a domestic dispute or some other situation-specific incident, it's rare to find a healthcare serial killer who selects not patients but other types of people as victims. In this chapter, we'll look at a female physician bent on obliterating her family (and several male physicians have done the same); we'll also examine the cases of a nurse who killed people so she could spend their money, a nurse who dismembered men he picked up, and a team of doctors who used their skills to facilitate lethal terrorism. Let's start with the nurse who liked to shop.

Dana Sue Gray, 36, entered an insanity plea in the Superior Court of Riverside, California on March 11, 1995. Two years earlier she had been charged with killing two people and attempting to kill yet a third woman. In addition, she remained a suspect in a third murder. She had known two of the victims and was traced via credit card use to the third. Stuart Sachs, Gray's public defender, stated that the mental problems from which Gray had suffered at the time of the murders were no longer an issue for her but had been significant factors in her past. Two psychiatrists evaluated her to affirm this, but the prosecutor, Richard Iey, had an expert who stated that Gray knew what she was doing at the time of the crimes. Iey expected to seek the death penalty.

Gray, a former operating room nurse at Inland Valley Medical Center, had beaten 66-year-old June Roberts with a wine bottle in Canyon Lake on February 28, 1995, and then strangled her with a telephone cord. Then two weeks later on March 16 she used both a rope and her hands to kill Dora Beebe, 87, of Sun City. Dora was found in a pool of blood from head injuries received while being hit with an iron. The weapons were left behind in the victims' homes. While investigating these crimes was difficult, a survivor of a similar attack during this time period was able to help.

Dorinda Hawkins, 57, identified Dana Sue Gray as the person who had entered her antiques shop on March 10 in Lake Elsinore. Gray had put a rope around Hawkins's neck and used the calming skill she had gained as a nurse to urge her to "just relax." Hawkins survived because she went limp and appeared to be dead.

Gray apparently wanted to use the victims' credit cards and gain access to their bank accounts to go on a spending spree. After killing them, she had forged their names on checks and used their cards to purchase items such as jewelry, liquor, shoes, spa services, and Western apparel. In fact, only three hours after Roberts' murder, Gray had used Roberts's credit card to buy lunch and get her hair restyled; those who encountered her said she had seemed cheerful; she even had a young boy with her. The investigation turned up $1,700 worth of purchases on the cards, charged on dates following Roberts's death. Gray had also withdrawn $2,000 from Beebe's bank account. Investigators believed that she had spotted Beebe at a shopping center and followed her home.

Once a successful registered nurse, Gray had lost her job, gone into bankruptcy, and suffered a divorce. Then she had a miscarriage and lost her home. Apparently, having all of these events occur in quick succession had put her under extreme stress. At one point, her savings account held only $100. Before the murder spree, Gray had abused alcohol and stopped taking her medication for depression (claiming a doctor had failed to properly monitor her), and that combination of factors became the heart of her insanity defense. At a news conference, Gray's half-brother described her as a woman with persistent financial problems and a spendthrift.

To avoid the death penalty and another murder charge in the future, Gray dropped her insanity defense in September 1998 and pled guilty to the charges of robbery, murder, and attempted murder. As she received life in prison, her attorney claimed that her remorse was sincere. Gray remarked, "My life and career has been focused on healing. I have strayed so far from that goal." Victims' families were unconvinced.

Gray remained a suspect in the stabbing and choking death of 87-year-old Norma Davis on February 14, who was her step-grandmother, but no charges were filed, based on a lack of physical evidence (although her shoes matched a footprint found at the home). Davis was stabbed 10 times, and aside from this modus operandi, the crime scene bore strong similarities to that of victim June Roberts. Gray also had a key to Davis's mobile home. This murder remains unsolved.[1]

Then there was the female physician who turned her lethal intent against her own family.

COLD-BLOODED

With different methods, Dr. Debora Green killed two of her children and tried killing her husband, Michael Farrar. An oncologist, Green lived with her husband, a cardiologist, and their three children in Prairie Village, Kansas. On October 24, 1995, their home went up in a roaring blaze as Green stood outside and watched. One child, Kate, jumped to safety, landing in her mother's arms, but 13-year-old Tim and 6-year-old Kelly failed to survive. They had been trapped on the second floor. Observers thought that Green's demeanor was remarkably calm for a woman who had just lost her home and two children, so an investigation took place, uncovering an unsavory tale of arson, adultery, and the attempt to obliterate a family.

Arson investigators found evidence of a liquid accelerant poured in various places inside the ruined house. Looking into Green's background, they discovered that her previous home had been similarly decimated by fire, shortly after she and her husband had separated. They had reunited, but the night before this recent fire, her husband had told her he wanted a divorce and custody of their children. They had been married for 18 years, although the relationship was rocky, thanks largely to Green's violent temper outbursts. Farrar had taken up with another woman, which Green had discovered. It wasn't long before Farrar was hospitalized with terrible stomach pains that nearly killed him. In fact, on the night of the fire, he was in the hospital for the third time, although by then he had moved out of the house.

The police searched Green's purse and found empty bags containing traces of castor beans, the source of the poison, ricin. Subsequent tests on Farrar's blood proved that he had ricin in his system. Comparing his activities just prior to his hospitalizations turned up information that each time Green had just served him a meal.

A month after the fire, the police charged Green with two counts of murder and two counts of attempted murder (her husband and her surviving daughter). In addition, they charged her with aggravated arson. She pled not guilty, but when she learned it was a death penalty case, she agreed to plead no contest in exchange for life in prison. In a statement to the court, she blamed alcohol abuse, her alleged psychiatric illness, and the lack of timely intervention.

In retrospect, Dr. Green decided that she should not have pled guilty, claiming that she was innocent of all charges. Given that she had been on several doses of medication at the time of the incidents, and under great stress, her new attorney stated in 2000 that she might not have been competent to make any legal decisions. But then she withdrew her motion for a new trial, for the same reason she had originally pled guilty. She remains in prison, with eligibility for parole.[2]

While Green was reacting to a situation, she was nevertheless acting with some degree of premeditation, ordering the castor beans and the accelerant that would burn down the house. Even people who are psychotic can be considered sane if they have an awareness that what they are doing is wrong. There was no indication that Green was so detached from reality that she could not comprehend the wrongness of her act, so whatever psychiatric illness she might have suffered, she still had the ability to comprehend what she was doing. Like many female killers, she targeted people close to her, but the next healthcare worker was a predator of strangers, in the classic manner of a serial killer.

LAST CALL

Along the rural East Coast during the early 1990s, the remains of five middle-aged men were found dumped along a major roadway, often in trash cans, where state workers picking up the trash discovered them. Dumped in Pennsylvania, New Jersey, and New York, each victim had been stabbed, dismembered, and wrapped tightly in several layers of plastic bags. From the method of cutting with a saw and a knife, wrapping, and disposal, it seemed to be the work of a single perpetrator, and he was soon dubbed the "Last Call Killer." But identifying this offender stymied police; despite more than 500 interviews by a dozen investigators and even an eyewitness who could identify the last person seen with one victim, all leads went cold. In part, that was because no physical evidence linked the best suspect to the killings. All of the men appeared to be either gay or bisexual, so that link was established, but they seemed to have no connection with each other. Seven years later, investigators learned about a unique new method, developed in Canada, for lifting fingerprints off plastic bags.

In 2000, the New Jersey State Police had sent around 50 plastic trash bags from the victims' remains to the Toronto Police Service for analysis via vacuum metal deposition. This involved using a gold-and-zinc process to produce a clear likeness of the prints, as the gold absorbed into the fingerprint residue. The zinc adhered to the gold to yield an image of the valleys between the ridges, and the print could then be photographed to make a permanent record. It took six months to process the bags, but identifiable fingerprints were lifted from several.

Still, they did not match anyone in the fingerprint databases. However in 2001, Maine went online with the Automated Fingerprint Identification System (AFIS), and among the prints in their database were those of Richard Rogers, Jr. In 1973, he had bludgeoned his graduate school roommate, Frederick Spencer, to death, but had been acquitted of the crime because his attorney convincingly argued self-defense. However, what caught the eye of investigators was Rogers's manner of disposal: He had bludgeoned Spencer with a hammer, then wrapped him in a plastic tent and dumped his corpse along the side of a road. More important, Rogers's fingerprints from that incident were a match to 36 fingerprints lifted from bags found on several of the Last Call Killer's victims. When police searched Rogers's apartment, they found a Bible with passages highlighted that involved decapitation and dismemberment.

The police arrested Rogers and charged him with the murder and dismemberment of the two victims found in New Jersey: the July 1992 homicide of Thomas Mulcahy, 57, a married bisexual business executive and father of four from Sudbury, Massachusetts, and the May 1993 killing of gay prostitute Anthony Marrero, 44, from Manhattan. For evidence, the police had fingerprints from the bags and fibers similar to those from carpets in Rogers's home. Gloves found on Mulcahey's body, yielding Rogers's prints, had been purchased on Staten Island where Rogers resided, which added to the circumstantial evidence, and two fingerprints and a palm print matching Rogers had been lifted from the bags wrapping this victim's parts.

Rogers's trial got underway on October 26, 2005 before Judge James N. Citta in Toms River, New Jersey. During jury selection, Rogers, 55, was offered a deal: plead guilty to manslaughter and receive two 30-year sentences with the possibility of parole in 15 years. Also, if he pled to third-degree murder in a case from Pennsylvania, he would be given 10 to 20 years in prison. Rogers agreed to consider it, but opted to go to trial. Judge Citta ruled that he would allow the prosecutor to discuss two similar murders from out of state.

Defense attorney David Ruhnke indicated that Rogers was innocent and claimed that his fingerprints on bags indicated only that he had carried something in them at some point in time, not that he had used them to wrap body parts. Other people's fingerprints had been found as well, which pointed to other possible suspects.

William Heisler, the assistant prosecutor and chief trial attorney for Ocean County, opened with witnesses who had discovered the bodies. Donald Giberson described how he came across a plastic bag on a dead-end dirt road on May 10, 1993 that proved to contain just a pair of arms. They were then traced to the missing Anthony Marrero, a known gay hustler from New York. Thomas Mulcahy's remains were found on July 10, 1992 in trash containers at two separate rest areas in Ocean and Burlington Counties. Marrrero's legs and torso were later found elsewhere. Medical Examiner Lyla Perez described the wounds to Mulcahy: After he was murdered by stabbing, his body was eviscerated and cut into seven separate parts. This bore similarities to other victims, also cut into seven parts.

There was also eyewitness testimony. A former bartender at the Five Oaks Bar in New York's Greenwich Village identified Rogers as the man she had seen with Michael Sakara, another victim. While Rogers is not on trial for his murder, Sakara's remains were found in a condition similar to the New Jersey victims. The bartender had seen Rogers with Sakara on July 30, 1993, and the following day, parts of Sakara's remains were found in Rockland County. He had been cut into seven pieces and packaged in plastic garbage bags. Sakara had introduced Rogers to the bartender, but had used a generic name. Yet she was aware that Rogers was a nurse and she picked him out of a set of photos the police had of male nurses in the area. That lead had not paid off then, but once the various prints from the bags were matched to Rogers, this woman became a valuable witness.

The circumstances supported the physical evidence and, altogether 35 fingerprints and two palm prints from all four cases had been identified from bags used to wrap the victims' parts. Mulcahy had disappeared after attending a business meeting in Manhattan and he'd been seen in a gay bar that Rogers frequented. There were 16 fingerprints matched to Rogers on bags that wrapped his remains. Marrero, a known gay hustler from Manhattan, was found killed, cut up, and also wrapped in plastic before being dumped in New Jersey. A palm print and two fingerprints linked him to Rogers. Peter Anderson, a victim found dismembered and dumped in Pennsylvania, was a gay man who had attended a meeting in Manhattan. A palm print and 18 fingerprints on the bags that wrapped his parts were matched to Rogers. Michael Sakara was seen with Rogers at a gay bar the evening before his body parts were found wrapped in several bags. In addition, Rogers's employment records from Mount Sinai Hospital in Manhattan indicated that he'd taken a few days off during times that coincided with each of the four murders.

Ruhnke called no witnesses on Rogers's behalf. Instead, he challenged the notion that Mulcahy and Marrero were killed in New Jersey and questioned the method used to lift the prints. Even if his client's fingerprints were on the bags, he reiterated, that fact was not proof that Rogers had committed murder.

What the jury had not heard, but reporters had described, were details about the case from 1973 in which Rogers had been acquitted of murder, as well as testimony about a fifth murder in Florida, that of Matthew Pierro, who had been discovered in 1982. While he was not dismembered, a bite mark on his body had been matched by an odontologist to Rogers. In addition, Rogers had been in Florida at the time and his fingerprints had been lifted from the crime scene. In this case, the man's heart had been removed.

The jury discussed the two cases for nearly four hours. During that time, they had sent out a panel to ask Judge James Citta again about jurisdiction issues. He indicated that New Jersey did have jurisdiction over the two cases, because the law allowed them to infer that if the bodies had been found in the state, the men had been killed there.

An hour later, they had a verdict. Although it was Friday evening, people filed back into the courtroom. The forewoman wept as she rose to announce their findings: Richard Rogers, 55, was guilty of the first-degree murder of Thomas Mulcahy and Anthony Marrero. He was also found guilty on two counts of hindering his apprehension by dismembering the victims and disposing of them the way he had.

Rogers showed no reaction. He simply stared at the front of the courtroom. Since the DA did not request the death penalty, Rogers received life in prison on each murder count, with no possibility of parole for at least 30 years, when he will be 85. Ruhnke announced that he would file an appeal. Rogers remains a suspect in the other three murders.[3]

APPEAL TO THE ELITE

Early on March 20, 1995, five members of the Aum Shinrikyo cult in Tokyo entered five different subway stations and boarded underground trains heading toward a central station near the National Police Agency headquarters. They sat quietly among the other passengers, holding their deadly packages and giving no hint as to what they were about to do, although they knew that some of the people they were touching and sitting next to would probably die. They didn't care. To them, the mission was more important than human life. Their leader had assured them that this was a holy mission. The more people who died that day by their hand, the better. It would advance the cult members' spiritual development.

At the agreed-upon moment, each assassin placed bags of the deadly nerve agent, sarin, on the floors of the trains, punctured them to release the gas, and disembarked. The fumes floated through the trains and into the stations, affecting over 5,000 commuters. Twelve people died that day and more than

50 were seriously harmed. Another thousand would suffer long-term effects. Yet the cult had hoped for even more victims.

Five days prior to this incident, this same group had attempted but failed to release botulinus bacteria, produced by the scientists among them. Their experiments with poisonous gas a year before—aimed at killing three judges scheduled to hear a lawsuit against them—had injured over 600 and killed 7. Their plan was to continue to poison people with more such incidents. In fact, they had stockpiled Ebola virus, chemical weapons, anthrax and explosives. Reports following several police raids stated that they had a sufficient amount of sarin gas to obliterate four million people.

The group counted among its members a number of prominent scientists and physicians, including Dr. Tomomasa Nakagawa, who had been instrumental in developing the sarin gas. Another was Dr. Ikuo Hayashi, a noted cardiologist.

Prior to joining Aum, Hayashi was a senior medical doctor at the Japanese Ministry of Science and Technology. He had graduated from Keio University, one of Tokyo's top schools, to become a heart specialist at Keio Hospital. He left there to become head of Circulatory Medicine at the National Sanatorium Hospital in Tokai, Ibaraki. But then in 1990, he resigned and abandoned his family to join Aum. Asahara appointed him the group's Minister of Healing, which included such duties as administering "special treatments" to suspected betrayers, such as sodium pentothal and electric shocks. Several Aum members died as a result.

Professional members not only had legal access to the substances and technology, but they were also protected against government inspections of their facilities, so they were able to work on their projects in secret. Cult members were suspected in numerous attacks on defectors and critics, many of whom died. They even had their own hospital in Tokyo where they could administer whatever form of torture they pleased. Some of their extreme ascetic practices and initiations killed even loyal members. The Japanese police surmised that between 1988 and 1995, the cult had killed 31 people and inspired two suicides.

After the attack on the subway, the police led a raid against the 25 known centers for this religion in Japan, to which the cult leaders responded with terroristic threats. They even attempted to release hydrogen cyanide into another subway station, but the device malfunctioned. It was estimated to have been lethal enough to have killed 20,000 commuters. Similar defective but potentially lethal devices were found at later times in the subways. Just in case, doctors in hospitals around the country prepared a defense with antidotes, aware that some of their former colleagues were in league with the devil.

During the investigative sweep, more than two hundred Aum practitioners were arrested, including the leading guru, Shoko Asahara, who was charged with 23 counts of murder and the production of illegal drugs. His various trials dragged on for years, but in February 2004, Asahara was given the death sentence for his part in over two dozen murders. His legal team appealed on the grounds that Asahara was mentally unfit. During a psychiatric examination, Asahara refused to speak, so the appeal failed. Eleven of his disciples received a similar sentence

At his trial, Dr. Ikuo Hayashi showed remorse for what he had done, as he reportedly wept in court. He said that he'd perceived in modern medicine a lack of spirituality, which he'd found in Buddhism. Then he'd met Asahara and had been so impressed with the man's apparent spirituality that he had brought his wife, also a medical doctor, and their children to live at the Aum compound in Yamanashi Prefecture. Hayashi claimed that he had genuinely believed that Asahara possessed supernatural powers. Despite witnessing the cult's nefarious activities, with drugs, weapons, and the outright murder of dissidents, he had accepted the notion that to save a disloyal member's soul, homicide was justified. Yet, he stated, he also had feared that if he did not do as he was told, he, too, might be killed. As he received a life sentence, Hayashi admitted that in this cult he had given up the ability to think for himself.

What inspires educated professionals to be drawn to such violent ideals? The Hindu word *Aum* means universe, and the rest of the name implies truth, faith, and reason. The route to the Final Realization involved a series of consciousness-elevating steps that supposedly made the practitioner superior to others, especially those perceived as ignorant and spiritually undeveloped. At the height of its power, the cult had at least 9,000 members in Japan alone, and large numbers of practicing groups worldwide. Its inspiring deity is in fact a god of destruction.

In *How the Millennium Comes Violently,* Catherine Wessinger indicates that the success of Aum was its appeal to intelligent, successful people who disliked the rigid conformity of Japanese society. The Aum cult made its members feel above all of that, enlightened via mystical experiences. For an even more in-depth analysis, Robert Jay Lifton studied the cult, following the examination he had made of the Nazi doctors, and in an interview, he discussed what he viewed as the "socialization to evil." Certain doctors would join a group that had a specific ideology that they appreciated, he said, especially if that group offered a biomedical vision and a means to revitalize their lives. If additionally, they took up residence in a camp or compound, they became isolated in a way that made it possible for them to absorb the ideology more fully into their day-to-day existence. The group leader, who strongly desired their membership, exposed them only gradually to the terror-istic aspects of the ideology and only after their loyalty, supported by fear, was already entrenched. Since they had found religious satisfaction early in their involvement, it was but a short psychological step for them to accept the jus-tifications the leader offered for killing. In the case of Aum, the doctors were encouraged to participate in the terror—and even threatened—by a talented con man, Asahara. As they achieved mystical experiences via meditation they were able to reframe their guru's ambitions as part of the spiritual vision. Thus, they seemingly became numb to the self-serving undercurrents of his call for violence.[4]

8

The Posers

STRANGLER

Some serial killers have pretended to be members of the healthcare industry, although they never had the credentials. This façade was their devious way of gaining access to people and falsely winning their trust. It's no surprise that a con artist would spot the opportunities inherent in pretending to have the prestigious social position, along with the elite knowledge and training, of a doctor. Failing that, pretending to be a nurse can yield similar benefits. There was also a serial killer who posed as a psychiatrist—a mental health expert with a medical degree. We'll turn first to that profile.

On October 17, 1977, a 19-year-old woman was picked up, strangled, and dumped near the entrance to Forest Lawn Hollywood Hills Cemetery in Los Angeles, California. This murder was followed by several more. The victims had often been bound and all were tossed away like trash. One young female, only 15, had been laid in a garden on an anthill with her legs posed in the shape of a diamond. It was clear that she had been trussed up with ligatures while alive and then strangled. A white fiber was found on her eyelid. Then two girls, 12 and 14, had been killed together and rolled down a 50-foot embankment into a trash heap. That same night produced a sixth victim, an art student, and her bruises matched those of the others. Then came an actress and a business student. Thousands of leads were called in and the media dubbed the killer the Hillside Strangler, but the police surmised that there were actually two offenders.

Another murdered prostitute was soon found naked on the side of a hill in plain view. She appeared to have been posed in a spread-eagle fashion, and this time someone had seen two males with her. However, the leads quickly dried up and no one was arrested. Nothing related to these cases occurred again until February 17, 1978, when a highway helicopter patrol spotted an orange car crashed off a highway. Locked inside the trunk was a woman who would become the tenth victim in the series of unsolved strangulation murders, although she'd been treated differently. It took a double homicide in another state to finally break the case.

In Bellingham, Washington, in January 1979, college roommates Diane Wilder and Karen Mandic went missing. One of them had told someone they were going to do a security job for Ken Bianchi, a good-looking captain at the security company with a girlfriend and infant son. The police questioned him, but he denied any knowledge of the girls. The radio stations aired a broadcast about them and their missing car, inspiring a woman to report such a car in a cul-de-sac. Inside the trunk, the police found the bodies of both girls. As they processed evidence, they realized that the girls had reported for their house-sitting job, so detectives returned to question Bianchi and search his residence. It turned out he had a hairbrush in which hair consistent with one of the victims was tangled. A pubic hair found on one girl resembled Bianchi's.

Since he had a California driver's license, detectives called the homicide division in Los Angeles and learned about the string of unsolved murders there. Bianchi's home had also produced jewelry from two of those victims. In addition, Bianchi had a cousin, Angelo Buono, who had an upholstery shop, and it was located not far from many of the spots where bodies had been dumped.

Both men were arrested for interrogation. However, Bianchi's attorney decided to hired a psychiatrist, Dr. John Watkins, to examine him. Watson put Bianchi under hypnosis, got him to admit to several of the murders and to implicate his cousin in others, and then declared that he had multiple personality disorder. He had killed as "Steve Walker" and was therefore not competent to stand trial. Three more experts were convinced as well. However, a background check indicated that "Steve Walker" was the name of a student from whom Bianchi had stolen college transcripts in order to get a fake degree. He had then set himself up in a fraudulent psychiatry practice, albeit short-lived. And he had clearly done his homework, because he could later malinger a mental illness so well he fooled several experts. No doubt, he had prepared himself in the event of an arrest.

Yet another psychiatrist tricked him into admitting he had faked it, and he then cut a plea deal in which he agreed to testify against his cousin in exchange for life in prison. (Still, he kept trying other mental illness angles.) He also pled guilty to the Washington murders and five of the Los Angeles murders. On Halloween in 1983, the jury convicted Buono of 9 of the 10 murders and gave him nine life sentences. Bianchi received five life sentences, and two in Washington. It's not easy to undergo hypnosis and successfully fake a disorder, but Bianchi clearly knew what he was doing. Fortunately, investigators caught on.[1]

In the next case, a self-claimed doctor lured young women into his "home office."

THE ACCOMMODATING "DOCTOR"

At number ten Rillington Place in London, England, the widowed tenant had left the downstairs flat, so the landlord allowed another tenant, Beresford Brown, to have temporary access to the kitchen. Brown noticed a foul odor, so he tried to eliminate it by cleaning. In the process, he decided to install a wall shelf for his radio. As he tested the walls to find a solid surface, he realized they were hollow, covered only by thin wallpaper. Hoping to find a cupboard, he pulled the paper away to reveal a closed door that was stuck. The odor seemed to come from behind it. Braun shone a light through the crack and was soon on his way to fetch the police.

Chief Superintendent Peter Beveridge took the coroner, Chief Inspector Percy Law from Scotland Yard, and a team of officers to Rillington Place. They pried open the door and found themselves looking at the bare back of a half-clothed dead woman. She had been decomposing in there for a while, and near this corpse was another large object, wrapped in a blanket. It proved to be tied with something that was knotted to the dead woman's bra. The body was removed to the living room to gain access to the package, and once she was out in the air, it was clear that she had been strangled with a ligature. Her hands were tied together in front of her.

Now that the team could see the package better, they noticed that deeper into this closet was yet another package, just as large. They pulled out the first one, unwrapped it, and knew before it was fully exposed that it was another body. Strangely, this woman's killer had stood her up on her head in the closet. The same proved true of the third wrapped package. All three bodies were sent to the morgue for autopsy while the flat was ordered off limits to all except official personnel involved in a search. Since they had noticed loose floorboards in the parlor, they pulled these up, dug into the loose rubble, and produced yet another female body. Number 10 Rillington Place was a veritable charnel house.

At the morgue, facts emerged about the victims' time since death. The first one, dead about a month, was in her twenties and from the color of her skin, it was evident that she had been administered carbon monoxide before being strangled. She had been sexually assaulted at, or just after, the time of her death. The second one removed from the closet had been dead about a month or two longer, and she, too, appeared to be in her mid-twenties and to have been gassed and strangled. She had also suffered sexual assault as she was dying and her remains exhibited several oddities: she wore only a cotton cardigan and vest, and another white vest had been placed between her legs in a diaper-like fashion. The third victim, the same age, had been six months pregnant, and had died from asphyxiation around the same time period as the second one. The fourth woman found—the one beneath the floorboards—was an older woman, probably 50, with several teeth missing. After being strangled, she had been rolled up in a flannel blanket, and her head was covered with a pillowcase. A silk nightgown and a flowered dress were wrapped around her and she appeared to have died three to four months earlier. Unlike the others, there were no signs of coal-gas poisoning or sexual intercourse. She had been strangled, probably by ligature.

The police went out looking for the former tenant, John Reginald Christie, or Reggie, who had left no forwarding address but was believed to be in London. In the meantime, an investigation turned up the identities of the victims. The woman buried under the parlor floor had been Ethel Christie, Reggie's wife. The others had been prostitutes whom he had apparently brought home to kill after Ethel was dead.

Other items in the house seemed related to the crimes: a man's tie in the closet, tied with a reef knot; potassium cyanide, and a tobacco tin containing four clumps of pubic hair, none of which matched the known victims. The house yielded little more of interest, but then police went into the garden. It did not take long to spot the human femur holding up a trellis. Digging produced more bones in the flower beds as well as some blackened skull bones with teeth. Nearby was a newspaper fragment dated July 19, 1943, and bits of fabric from a dress. Although only one skull was unearthed, the remains of at least two women were in this garden. After reconstruction, painstaking processing of clues, and the examination of records of missing women, they identified both victims.

But the police were concerned about two more victims. Several years earlier the wife and infant daughter of the former upstairs tenant, Timothy Evans, were murdered. At the time, he had accused Christie of these deeds, but the police had believed Christie's denials and Evans was convicted and executed. Investigators now wondered, had they been mistaken?

Christie was wandering around London neighborhoods, booking rooms and basically waiting to be caught. As he ran out of money, he slept on park benches. On the last day of March, a police officer spotted him and took him to the Putney Police station, where he gave his detailed statement.

One day in a bar, he said, he encountered a 21-year-old Austrian girl named Ruth Fuerst. She became his lover, meeting with him whenever his wife was away. One day when they were in bed, a telegram arrived to announce that Ethel was on her way home. Rather than be caught, Christie strangled Fuerst and stashed her body under the floorboards in the front room. Later he moved it to the garden. The girl's disappearance was reported to the police on September 1, but her whereabouts remained a mystery.

It was not long before Christie met his second victim, Muriel Eady, 32. He often invited her for tea, served by his wife, and learned about some physical ailments from which she suffered. In October 1944, when Christie was alone one day, Muriel came over. Christie had told her that, due to his background in first-aid with the War Reserve, he had a remedy for her physical problems, so she wanted to be treated. But he had a devious plan. Before she arrived, he'd placed some inhalant into a jar, disguising it with the odor of friar's balsam. He had made two holes in the top of the jar, one of which he used for a small hose that he ran to the gas supply. That tube ran into the liquid and another tube came out the other hole, meant to keep the concoction from smelling like gas. When Muriel arrived, Christie had her sit on a kitchen chair with a scarf over her head. He instructed her to take a deep breath.

As she expanded her chest, she inhaled carbon monoxide. It weakened her, which gave Christie the opportunity to strangle her with a stocking. All the while, he had sex with her, apparently excited by his complete control over her. Since she had no fresh air supply, she quickly expired and he placed her body in the communal washhouse while he dug a hole for her in the garden. It was her femur, surfacing later, which had propped up the trellis.

Of his wife, Christie claimed that her choking had awakened him and he'd tried but failed to restore her breathing. Unable to bear her suffering, he used a stocking to strangle her. He then found a bottle that had contained phenal-barbitone tablets, prescribed for his insomnia, which was now nearly empty and he realized Ethel had committed suicide. He said she had been depressed over the new tenants, whom she viewed as persecuting her. Saddened by his loss, Christie had placed her corpse in the floor to keep her nearby.

The statement was self-serving and unlikely, but the police allowed Christie to keep talking, because they wanted to know about the victims he had placed into a closet. He said he had killed Rita Nelson in January when she said she would accuse him of sexual assault if he didn't give her some money. In his house, they had struggled and she fell back on a chair that happened to have a rope hanging from it. Christie claimed he'd blacked out and woken up with her strangled. Then he wrapped her up and shoved her into the cupboard. Ten days later, he met Kathleen Maloney in a café and sat at a table where two girls were looking for flats. He suggested his place, and Kathleen came by. When she became aggressive, he stated, he defended himself and she, too, ended up in the closet. He told a similar story about the third girl, Hectorina Maclennan, although he claimed her death had been "accidental."

The facts belied the tale Christie told, but that was for the courtroom to sort out. He was arrested and detained, while several psychiatrists examined him. The police wanted him to talk about the murders of Timothy Evans's wife Beryl and their child, but Christie initially refused to admit them. Then he reluctantly said he had accidentally murdered Beryl by trying to perform an abortion (although investigators believed he had probably tried to have sex with her, in his typical manner). He still insisted that Evans had killed the child.

Christie stood trial that June on the charge of murdering Ethel, and he pled not guilty by reason of insanity. His attorney brought in all of the other murders and called his client a maniac and madman. Dr. Jack Abbott Hobson, a psychiatrist for the defense, concurred. He said Christie was a severe hysteric who may have known what he was doing at the time of each murder but had a mental defect and thus did not appreciate that his acts were wrong.

The prosecution team had two experts to rebut this observation: Dr. J. M. Matheson and Dr. Desmond Curran. Dr. Matheson said that Christie had a hysterical personality but not a defect of reason that would prevent him from appreciating the nature of his acts. Dr. Curran found likewise, and the prosecutor then provided behavioral evidence that the things that Christie had done to avoid detection after killing his wife were indicative of full awareness of the wrongful nature of his acts.

The defense attorney responded to this by asking the jury to consider how abominable Christie's actions were: having intercourse with dying or dead women; collecting pubic hairs from victims; living, eating, and sleeping with those bodies nearby; how could he be sane? An acquittal, he insisted, was the only correct response.

After only an hour and twenty minutes, the jury found Christie to be guilty and sane. He was sentenced to death. Christie did not appeal and there were no medical grounds for reprieve, so in short order, on July 15, 1953, he was hanged at Pentonville Prison. In 1966, after a great deal of controversy over the possibility that the state had executed an innocent man, Timothy Evans received a posthumous pardon.[2]

Now let's look at a couple of women who faked their medical credentials.

CON ARTIST

Several nurses have viewed the area of patient care as a way to con people out of their money. One of the cleverest was Amy Archer-Gilligan, the inspiration for the 1940s Broadway hit about two elderly female poisoners, *Arsenic and Old Lace*. Although she had no education in the field or other qualifications, Archer-Gilligan billed herself as a nurse in 1901, when she and her husband James Archer opened a nursing home for the elderly in Newington, Connecticut. They took over the house and grounds of an aging man in need of care, and then took in other patients. Amy claimed to know a lot about medicine and people believed her, especially since she said she had trained at New York's Belleview Hospital.

In 1907, the Archers moved 10 miles away to Prospect Street in Windsor, Connecticut, opening the Archer Home for the Elderly and Infirm, with 14 beds. These were the first such private institutions of this kind in the country, and the latter especially received a great deal of community support. In Windsor, Amy partnered with a local doctor, Howard Frost King, also the medical examiner, to assist with getting medications and signing death certificates when needed. She was careful to give out stories of how difficult it was to care for people who were so terribly ill, because when they died, no one questioned it.

Her devoted patients ("inmates") called her Sister Amy, due to her outward pose as a good Christian woman, and she usually dressed in a checkered shirt and a solemn black skirt. To make money, Amy (and possibly her husband) came up with a much more profitable scheme. "Sister Amy" persuaded her patients to pay an insurance premium of $1,000, for which she promised them lifetime care, no matter how long they lived. This lump sum saved relatives from having to remember to make monthly payments. It seemed too good to be true and many jumped at the chance. Once she had the money in her possession, Amy ensured that they took up no more of her resources. Smothering or poisoning them, she explained their deaths to Dr. King as old age.

He apparently saw no reason to be suspicious, despite the rising death toll at Sister Amy's small facility, and he continued to sign off on each fatality. Between 1911 and 1916, there were 48 deaths, and in fact, both of Sister

Amy's successive spouses had died, too, one of them within three months of marrying her and shortly after he made out his will in her favor.

James Archer died on February 10, 1911, leaving behind one daughter. His diagnosis was Bright's Disease and Amy had been his bedside nurse. In fact, she assured everyone that those who died at the home had received the best of care and would have had no complaints. Each death, she told others, made her sad, and she pretended that the funeral expenses for those whose families were gone came out of her pockets. The truth was, she had collected this money from the patients or families ahead of time.

Amy was nearly ruined by a lawsuit in 1909, but was soon back on her feet, making money. A few patients complained to relatives of poor treatment and crowded facilities, but these tales were either ignored or quickly hushed.

By 1914, authorities were growing suspicious, so an undercover officer signed himself into Sister Amy's nursing home. He listened to her spiel and collected evidence of fraud, and then took his findings to his colleagues. Despite Amy's denials of wrong-doing, officials exhumed the bodies of Amy's second husband and some of her former patients. Finding high doses of arsenic in the body tissues, they charged Amy Archer-Gilligan with six counts of murder. Consulting with physicians, they discovered that an average annual death toll in such a small place would be 8 to 10, not 48 (although with few such facilities available for comparison, there was little basis for their estimates). Yet authorities wondered, how could Dr. Howard not have noticed? He'd seen the crowded conditions and had commented on the fact that people were not getting the quality of care for which they had paid.

Amy's defense was that most of the people sent to this place had been elderly, frail, and in declining health. They were a burden to others, expected to die. Oddly, Dr. King, who had failed time and again to record details about the patients' illnesses and causes of death, sided with Amy, apparently accepting the notion that the poison found had been planted in those bodies to frame her.

Archer-Gilligan stood trial in 1917 for the murder of Franklin Andrews. He had been in good health upon moving in and had accepted the assurance that he would be comfortable there. He turned over $1,000 and lived at the facility for over a year. During that time, he noticed that patients around him were dying from no apparent cause. He'd begun to document these incidents in letters to relatives, including the death of Amy's second husband, Michael Gilligan, who was apparently in good health. Prior to his demise, Andrews was also under duress from Amy's bullying as she tried to get him to give her a sizable loan and he noticed that she had done the same with other patients, who then had died. Andrews feared for his life. Just before Andrews died,

Amy had assured someone on the waiting list that a bed would soon be available—and his was the only bed she could have meant. The totality of circumstances was against her. The prosecutor suggested that Amy fed many of her patients arsenic via spiked warm lemonade—her typical "remedy"—and records supported her multiple purchases of the poison.

Amy's pitiful defense amounted to this: She was a good Christian, which prohibited her from doing such things. The evidence against her was strong, however, and she was convicted and given the death penalty. But she appealed and won a second trial. Avoiding another sensational legal proceeding, she pled guilty and received a life sentence. Amy insisted that she would do everything in her power to prove her innocence and clear her name, but she ended up serving her sentence in an institution for the insane, while her former residence was dubbed the "Death House" and "Murder Factory." She died in 1962.[3]

CAPITAL CRIMES

Another nurse, Anna Marie Hahn, had a similar idea, but she pursued it more like a grifter. She had arrived from Germany in 1927, when she was 21, and settled in Cincinnati, Ohio. There she began to administer live-in healthcare to several elderly wealthy men, ingratiating herself into their wills. By 1932, she had acquired one estate from the deceased Ernest Koch and was taking what she could from the homes of two other patients who had died. Since the final hours of these men had not been easy, word came to the police that there was something suspicious going on. An investigation was launched in 1937 and the body of the latest victim, George Obendoerfer, was exhumed.

It turned out that Hahn had used arsenic and a strong purgative to dispatch her charges. A search of her home revealed a cabinet full of poisons, which led to the exhumation of her other patients. It turned out that she had used different substances for each victim, and she was charged with the murders of five men.

At the trial, Hahn attempted to turn her profiteering into missions of mercy, claiming that her former employers had been ailing, so she had assisted them to die. Yet records indicated that each man had been in good health, not likely to die and certainly not suffering. Then Hahn's former husband turned on her, telling the court that she had tried to persuade him to insure his life for a large amount of money. He refused and was soon suffering from severe stomach cramps. Believing she was out to get his assets, he had divorced her.

While Hahn admitted to swindling and theft, she claimed to be innocent of the murders. Yet the jury convicted her and on June 20, 1938, she became Ohio's first female to be executed in the electric chair.[4]

THE MIRACLE WORKER

Hu Wanlin was a Sichuan native of China. While serving a sentence in jail for intentional homicide, swindling, and abducting and trafficking in women, he decided to open a medical practice. He had only a basic education and no professional training, but he freely treated fellow inmates. When released from prison, Wanlin continued to practice fraudulent medicine in the Shaanxi and Henan provinces. It was not difficult to find patients, especially since he gave it added flourish.

Wanlin called himself a miracle-worker, claiming he could diagnose patients with only a cursory examination. He worked in the traditional practice of *qigong,* which requires the healer to emit energy in the form of *qi* from his body. The *qi* would have curative powers, without needing to have physical contact. There were thousands of such practitioners in China, with eager followers, but Wanlin stood out. When he became a public figure, offering documentation of his miracles, scientists denounced him. They were aware that he sold home-made herbal medicines mixed with the mineral salt mirabilite, thus giving patients lethal amounts of sodium sulfate. It was no surprise to them that some patients died from his treatments.

Finally arrested in January 1999 at the age of 50, Wanlin was suspected of causing the deaths of nearly 150 patients. Ultimately, he was charged with illegally practicing medicine and was convicted of three murders, receiving a prison sentence of 15 years. He also had to pay a substantial fine and he lost his right to vote for five years.[5]

This case helped bring attention to the problems China has had with unauthorized medical practice, and China has now set up a medical system under which only licensed doctors are allowed to treat patients.

So now we've examined a selection of doctors, nurses, and other health-care workers, both legitimate and fraudulent, and have noted the diversity of methods and circumstances in which such killers practiced. Let's now list the most common motives and define the warning signals for those who work with HCSKs, employ them, or might be treated by them, with an eye toward thwarting their ability to kill in a healthcare setting.

9

Reasons that Become Red Flags

THE PROFILE

There is no way to provide a generic profile of HCSKs, because each case, while exhibiting common behaviors and contexts, is nevertheless unique. Some experts believe that attempting a profile based on a psychological and behavioral blueprint is risky, as it could result in selective attention to stereotypical details and neglect of distinctive indicators, but others believe there is sufficient overlap in these cases to at least devise a reasonable risk assessment. In this chapter we look at the motives of HCSKs, which inspired certain behaviors that offer us a collection of red flags common to a high percentage of them. In the following chapter, we'll list these warnings and discuss what healthcare facilities can do (and are doing) as the result of HCSKs in the system. Despite denial and disbelief—the ally of any HCSK—the increase in these cases over the past four decades has made it necessary to take firm steps to stop them.

These days, especially in technologically developed countries, it's more difficult for HCSKs to operate freely because with the use of computer tracking and surveillance systems, victim tolls and the depletion of drugs stand out more conspicuously. In addition, many nurses are trained in forensic investigation, so they better understand the need to be observant and to document. We know more about how these people operate, too, because we have better awareness about serial killers in general. There's no reason to believe that hospitals and other healthcare facilities would be immune from predatory killers, since they show up in many types of venues.

HCSKs are usually predators, whether due to having an evil character or a less malignant personality disorder. As such, they learn how to use the most subtle means of murder and gain access to pharmaceuticals without being detected. Unless some specific behavior triggers suspicion, they may effectively hide their crimes for quite a long time. As mentioned in the introduction, HCSKs generally use some sort of overdose, equipment tampering, or smothering, and they are quick to claim when apprehended that their motives were mercy or compassion. In most cases, evidence undermines this claim. Let's examine the genuine motives in more detail.

The Desire to Be a Hero

Some HCSKs, both male and female, look for ways to turn a medical case into a dramatic emergency in which they play the lead role. Even if the person dies, they appear to try as hard as they can to be the rescuer, which wins accolades from colleagues and staff. They also like taking command of the situation, yelling orders at others—especially those who outrank them. It matters little to them that the patients might die, as we've learned from those who were caught. Richard Angelo, for example, said he just wanted to feel better about himself. To him, the medical emergency was like being a fireman. Genene Jones seemed to enjoy putting children into cardiac arrest so she could pretend to use all possible means to revive them, as did Daisuke Mori and Benjamin Geen. Closely aligned with this is another motive—the need for attention.

Attention

In some cases, nurses who kill are seeking attention and may have developed a personality disorder known as Munchausen syndrome by proxy; most such nurses are female, but it's not unheard of in a male. People with this disorder know how to lie easily and in great detail and to disguise what they're doing to allay suspicion. What happens to their charges is not their concern; they're in it for their own needs.

But some HCSKs without this disorder have also enjoyed the attention, evident in their confessions once they're caught. Charles Cullen's agreement to be interviewed by detectives without an attorney, for example, coupled with his quick and shocking confession, suggests that he wanted the full extent of what he did to be known: it may be that, having been caught, he wanted to show how clever he was. The length of his initial interview—seven hours—also affirmed this, as did how much he repeated information about his circumstances and "poor me" state of mind. In fact, while he offered to confess to all his murders, he did not even make it to his claimed minimum of 30, let alone 40.

Donald Harvey, too, confessed to many more murders than his official toll credits, as did Efren Saldivar. It's difficult to know with those seeking attention whether they might be lying just to make their cases more dramatic and media-worthy. Sometimes serial killers wish to become known for having the most victims, so they will study other cases in order to claim more than the current record-holder. It's important for investigators not to take the confessions of HCSKs at face value, because HCSKs have recanted confessions, leaving investigators with nothing.

Experimentation

Some people go into healthcare because they're innately curious about the human body, and the only way to experiment with it without being discovered is to harm or kill the victims. H. H. Holmes was a good example, as was Joseph Mengele (although as a Nazi during Hitler's regime he did not have to find ways to cover it up). Michael Swango, too, experimented on patients, as did Jane Toppan, and it's likely that even when other motives are dominant, experimenting with substances proves interesting to a high percentage of HCSKs. This is especially evident with those killers who use a variety of methods, rather than sticking to one that clearly works.

Thrill

For some HCSKs, committing a violent death can be as exciting as a sexual encounter. They seek the heightened feeling that comes from the excitement that results from killing or watching others react to a death. H. H. Holmes and Marcel Petiot both had special rooms and peepholes for watching their victims die. Michael Swango described a major fatal accident as an ultimate fantasy and admitted that he loved emerging from the ER with an erection, knowing he was about to inform parents their child was dead. Genene Jones found this experience exciting, as did Kristen Gilbert, while team killers Gwendolyn Graham and Catherine Wood clearly derived an erotic thrill from their so-called Murder Game.

Power or Control

It takes little imagination to appreciate that people are attracted to medical care because they enjoy or seek power. It's no surprise that males might have this goal, given their biological drive to dominate, but researcher Carol Anne Davis states that many female killers feel empowered as well when they get away with murder. Dominant women intent on violence, she says, tend to be sexually driven, narcissistic, secretive, and manipulative. Often victimized in some manner during their lives, they turn this situation around by victimizing others. It feels good to them to dominate.[1] Genene Jones certainly felt protected by her superiors, and when she added her ability to generate attention and to get away with murder for several years, she seemed to develop a sense of invincibility. She had power over not just her patients but also those with whom she worked: she could charm some of them into siding with her, which left her free to do what she wanted.

Some killers have said that to take a human life makes them feel like God, with power over life and death. The driving force behind such murders is the need for outright control, girded with the killer's belief that he or she is special in some superior way. *The Diagnostic and Statistical Manual of Mental Disorders, 4th Edition (DSM-IV-TR)* includes narcissistic personality disorder (NPD) in Cluster B on Axis II, with three other disorders that can manifest in egocentric behavior. A personality disorder is a persistent pattern of maladaptive behavior that causes dysfunction in relationships or at work. While not all people with NPD are criminals, NPD is commonly found among serial killers. They feel entitled to their victims and their self-involved arrogance contributes to their sense of personal importance. They might even be narcissistic in the extreme form found in psychopathy, which is discussed in further detail below.

Having an approving or submissive partner also energizes those seeking power, making them feel even more grandiose. Waltrud Wagner in Austria is a good case in point, as is the team of Wood and Graham.

True of both genders, once caught, HCSKs attempt to manipulate the system, still believing in their own power. Sometimes they even succeed, getting an acquittal or lesser sentence. Their confessions often reveal their sense of superiority.

Necrophilous Voyeurism

This motive has not been mentioned on other researchers' lists, but it's worth consideration. Psychoanalyst Erich Fromm defines "necrophilism" as an attitude that can produce "malignant aggression." People influenced by this perspective hold a set of values that make them embrace death over life, which manifests in a craving for control and a desire to avoid the unpredictable nature of life. But it's more than that: it also involves a malignant aggression rooted in the desire to make a distinctly destructive mark on one's world. Such people are driven by a yearning for life to finish itself and they often have dreams about dismembered parts or rooms full of rotting remains. For them, killing another person is the ultimate form of control. They cannot relate well to living people and have a keen interest in sickness and an insensitivity to tragedy involving loss of life.[2]

A number of HCSKs enjoyed not just the event of causing a fatal emergency but also the effects on others. They might remain in the room to listen to the family members console one another or get into discussions with other staff members about the deceased patient. They might also reveal their own fantasies and dreams about death, as Michael Swango did to colleagues. A necrophilous character is attracted to the manifestations of death and in the most malignant form, will cause it and then enjoy its aftermath.

Relief from Inner Conflicts

Several HCSKs have been evaluated by psychologists or psychiatrists as acting out against others to gain relief from the stress of their inner turmoil or depression. However, one does not kill just because one hurts—or we would all be out there killing people. There's a reason that the HCSK chooses that particular way of dealing with his or her issues, as well as why they not only continue to do it but eventually feel driven to. Charles Cullen and Donald Harvey are both prime examples, but Beverly Allitt, too, was thought to be channeling her personal issues into acts of murder. Then there was Marcel Petiot, who claimed a history of mental instability for some of his acts. Among the various kinds of inner conflicts HCSKs experience includes a fear of losing control.

Fear of Loss of Control

It's possible that some HCSKs have developed from childhood experiences into adults who need to exert control over their worlds; this is true of many adult children of alcoholics who had experienced the insecurity of an unpredictable parent, as well as of children who have lost a parent to death. Charles Cullen lost his father at a young age and his mother when he was in high school; Harold Shipman took care of his mother as she died. It's possible that as they began to kill patients, they found some measure of relief from anxiety when they exercised this form of control—not just over another person but also over their environments. But perhaps the compulsion emerged years earlier.

Predatory Challenge/Addiction

Beyond the category of thrill is a compulsion to beat the system or measure oneself against each new safeguard. The excitement of this can be addictive, often deriving from the fusing of challenge with erotic development. An individual finds some item or act to be stimulating and the brain responds with pleasure, rewarding an approach to the exciting object or act. But the person eventually grows bored and seeks more such stimulation. Eventually, however, he will feel empty again and the cycle will repeat, further strengthening the erotic charge and inspiring the desire for a higher high. The behavior can escalate and perhaps involve more intensity or violence, usually from setting up greater challenges or risks. Erotic enthrallment with harm to others for one's own gratification starts with environmental opportunities and associations and becomes stronger via acts that stimulate the brain's reward mechanisms. The neural reward system processes these behaviors in a way that ensures repetition.[3]

Many HCSKs become addicted to the rush of anticipation, the energy of finding a way to put patients at risk or "out of their misery," and the exhilaration of those moments when the HCSK realizes that he or she has gotten away with such an act. This pattern has been true of many serial killers. The victims matter less and less (during his confession Cullen said they were all in a fog and he could barely remember them), and the experience becomes increasingly more gratifying, so that the activity tends to escalate into greater intensity and frequency.

Disdain

The way people treat the objects of their violence speaks to how they feel about people in general. A number of nurses who've been caught exhibit poor self-esteem. They may feel so inadequate that harming others or setting up a risky situation is the only way they view themselves in terms of worth. Their disdain for the patient often mirrors their disdain for themselves. This could come from abuse as a child or the failure to be accepted by peers. Yet some are just narcissistic snobs; Shipman's derisive labels for his patients is a prime example. If a HCSK fails to recognize human worth, he can more easily snuff others out.

Perverted Compassion

Several nurses have claimed that their fatal injection or asphyxiation of patients was done out of a sense of mercy. In fact, there is a case about which this might actually be true. A 24-year-old nurse in Budapest, Timea Faludi, who was known as the Black Angel because she always wore black, was suspected in the deaths of 37 patients over the span of a year, although she was convicted in 2001 of only 7. In her confession, she said she wished to "ease her terminally ill patients into death." The patients were in fact quite ill and in pain, as far as the sparse details of the story reveal, with no hope of recovery; they were on the terminally ill ward. However, so-called mercy-killing has often been a cover for other dark motives, and in any event, it's no justification for making the decision to take another person's life.

Paula Lampe, a former nurse and author of *The Mother Teresa Syndrome*, has collected information about HCSKs for several years. Since 1970 in Holland alone, she counts four male and five female HCSKs, while around the world she has looked at 81 cases. In her books, she discusses what she believes is a fine line between aggression and the desire to be needed. Those caregivers with self-esteem issues and other personal needs, she says, might cross the line into murder. She believed that Martha U, for example, did not murder to help others but to end her own unbearable feelings of "transparency." The "helping" aspect was actually a dangerous compulsion that carried with it a secret sense of power: "I have killed someone and nobody knows."

Within this framework, Lampe also discusses Shipman, Saldivar, Graham and Wood, and a male nurse in Germany, Rudi Paul Zimmerman, who was convicted during the 1970s of three murders and four counts of attempted murder in a hospital and a home for the elderly. He was also charged with serious abuse and received a life sentence.

Ease the Workload/Laziness

Several nurses have revealed this motive, although not until after they first—or simultaneously—claimed mercy. Efren Saldivar is perhaps the most notorious and cavalier example of nurses who killed to make their jobs easier, but a number of nurses, such as Andermatt and Majors, described a similar situation. Barbara Salisbury in England, convicted of two attempted murders but suspected in several actual ones, offered a defense that she was pressured to free up beds. The idea that they might kill people just because they're tired and overworked (or lazy) reveals a complete lack of awareness of their victims' worth. This motive, like disdain, is a far cry from what a nursing career is about. Kristin Gilbert even "facilitated" a death so she could leave early.

Profit

Some doctors participate in schemes to defraud insurance companies by killing people and sharing in the death benefits. Dr. Morris Bolber organized a partnership for this type of crime in Philadelphia in the 1930s. It is estimated that he and his partners killed around 50 people before they were stopped. The St. Louis dentist, Glennon Engleman, had a similar scheme, with a lesser victim toll but equally deadly intentions. The study by Yorker and colleagues includes two sets of HCSKs, one in Poland and one in Russia, that could be responsible for up to 4,000 deaths because they were in a financial arrangement with the funeral or organ harvesting industry. Thus far, there are few details about them.

Making Colleagues Look Bad

A few HCSKs either cited the desire to make colleagues look bad or allegedly mentioned this as a reason why they put patients at risk, even to the point where they died. Petr Zelenka admitted to doing so, and this was the motive attributed to Mario Jascalevich in New Jersey. It's likely that this is at least a secondary motive as well for nurses who feel disempowered by the healthcare hierarchy. In East Germany during the 1970s, Fritz Rudloff, a male nurse, killed the patients of the hospital director as payback for discipline. He used arsenic on four men admitted for various procedures simply to ruin his boss's reputation. They all died and an investigation revealed the poison in their systems. It was a risky game, and in the end Rudloff was convicted and executed.

PERSONALITY DYNAMICS

Forensic psychiatrist Dr. Robert Kaplan was interviewed on a radio program in England shortly after reports about Harold Shipman's growing list of victims. He compared Shipman to Hitler, since both had lost their mothers during their adolescence and both were quite distraught over it. Kaplan suggested that extreme grief at a vulnerable age can play a part in the development of aggression later in life, especially if they develop a pathological need to exert control. Yet such killers, he states, can have any sort of background, including one with no overt trauma or abuse.

Kaplan noted that there are two basic theories about serial killing physicians: (1) as predators, medicine attracts them because it gets them close to their interest in life and death; and (2) initially ordinary physicians become serial killers because they learn how to do it, have the means, and find it easy.

Either way, they tend to be self-obsessed and convinced of their own superiority and moral rectitude. When they get away with murder, they develop a sense that they can do as they please. If patient was wealthy, their funds "should" be transferred to benefit the physician.

Kaplan also addressed the issue of anger. The logic of a HCSK is that because life is unfair, they'll make others pay. As emotionally detached as a HCSK might be, anger can always drive them. Shipman could have been angry over his mother's death, for example, carrying it around and acting out against patients, who were easy targets. It might be true that medical training that encourages clinical detachment could suppress strong emotions to the extent that their energy builds and demands some sort of expression. Some doctors will choose aggression against easy targets.[4]

Robert Jay Lifton is an American psychiatrist known for his studies on political violence, thought reform, and what he calls the "protean self." He believed that the human personality is fluid and multi-faceted, and can be shifted under the pressure of situational demands. To participate in something like murder, he argues that doctors must possess the psychological mechanism that allows it. In his book, *The Nazi Doctors,* which is an attempt to explain what occurred in Nazi Germany with professionals who would not ordinarily kill, Lifton proposes the notion of "doubling." It's generalizable to any type of professional who must develop a clinical distance.

According to Lifton, a person is capable of existing as two independently functioning wholes so that a "part-self" can act as an entire self, each part surfacing according to the demands of the situation. This is not dissociative identity disorder in which the person has two functional personalities, nor a schizophrenic psychosis. Doubling is instead an adaptive mechanism that under certain conditions can assist any of us to survive, but it can also serve nefarious purposes.

Doctors or nurses who double in order to kill use their clinical distance as a way to redistribute their sense of morality to accommodate their killing. To some extent, they're aware of what they're doing but they fail to consider the meaning of their deeds. Ironically, Cullen claims he killed because patients were being "dehumanized"—as if by killing them he did not also discount their humanity. Self-consistency is not high on the doubler's list. They possess no sense of integrity, and each part of the doubled self acts according to its own situational demands and opportunities. In fact, many HCSKs are quick to claim they're being victimized.

The doubled self is responsible for what it does, and if murder becomes necessary in their minds, or desirable, then it can be reinterpreted in such a way as to ensure that it be repeated. Doubled doctors or nurses can view themselves as compassionate and humane, yet still go out and kill.

Depending on the person involved, Lifton describes three types of doubling: The limited doubler kills only under certain permissible circumstances, such as financial or personal need; the conflicted doubler feels guilty but still kills; and the enthusiastic doubler is pleased to know that he can kill, get away with it, and still function normally. Lifton states that only psychopathic individuals can double for long periods without emotional harm, and it is the psychopathic individuals that are enthusiastic doublers. In fact, psychopaths suffer no remorse and have no trouble killing to achieve their personal goals, as often as they can.[5]

To review, most serial killers are psychopaths, which means they are narcissistic, impulsive, and callous, with a tendency to divert blame from themselves to others. From brain scan studies, it appears that they fail to process the emotional content of situations, such as empathy, concern, or alarm, and tend to seek arousal. Their offenses are more brutal than those of other criminals, more aggressive and more diverse. They also represent a high percentage of repeat offenders. They're resistant to therapy and intolerant of frustration. It doesn't matter whom they hurt; what matters is that they get what they can for themselves. They find victims easily because they're glib, charming, and predatory, while their victims are generally trusting, vulnerable, and naïve. Psychopaths don't suffer from fear of consequences because unless it's immediate and severe, the idea of punishment has little impact on them.

A large percentage of the nurses appeared to show no feelings of remorse for what they did or to have any concern about the people they killed. In most cases, there were no apologies to families of the deceased. In fact, many psychopaths roam free in society—approximately one out of 100—and for those who feel compelled to kill, what better place to do it without discovery than a facility where people die anyway? They're generally good at charming themselves into a position and at hiding their intentions. While guilt and remorse are not part of their emotional repertoire, they do feel anger, even rage, and they take it out on the most vulnerable people. Some kill just for the physical charge it gives them, which may derive from the depressed autonomic system that psychopaths apparently have.

Another idea, which complements Lifton's concept, comes from Dr. Al Carlisle, a psychologist at Utah State Prison. He describes a serial killer as having a "compartmentalized" self: a public persona that appears to others to be adaptive and a darker side that allows murderous fantasies free reign. Such Jekyll/Hyde personalities evolve from childhood. Some children have painful memories from abuse, disappointment, frustration, or being bullied, and to escape they utilize comforting fantasies in which they exact revenge. The more they indulge, the more they round out an alternate identity that allows them to feel more powerful; however, such fantasies can turn violent and they eventually seek release. An opportunity to act out can provide the right conditions to turn a fantasizer into a killer.

As with Lifton's doubler, the compartmentalized killer allows the expression of unacceptable impulses, desires, and aspirations to become an equal with his or her more appropriate persona. Then as normal life grows more boring, frustrating, or disappointing, the powerful and unrestricted fantasy life becomes more attractive. Eventually, with mental rehearsal, the brutal dimension gains greater substance and unrestricted fantasy feeds an unquenchable habit.

Killers who get away with their acts often learn the best ways to deflect others from discovering their secrets. They can speak convincingly about socially approved venues of right and wrong, even knowing that they commit evil acts. Their secret lives grow darker, supported by a private moral logic, and they can maintain a high level of functioning even while they think about murder and actively seek victims. The effort to keep the fantasies about death separate from normal daydreams forms a boundary that makes them distinct, but the more the fantasies are suppressed, the more energy they gain, especially if the person's so-called normal side has little ego strength or integrity.

Acting out the fantasy can feel powerful or satisfying as it displaces remorse, self-hate, or guilt. With no effective inhibitions, the hunt for victims begins again. When it becomes overly compulsive, it can psychologically overwhelm the killer, leading to decompensation, carelessness, and mistakes.[6] Many HCSKs grow bolder and more daring, taking greater risks, and thus often they make the mistakes that alert others to their spate of murders.

TEAM KILLERS

Most HCSKs are loners, but as we have seen, some have teamed up, finding willing accomplices—sometimes quite a few. In studies of team killers, researchers have found that many pairings follow a common pattern: two or more people meet, feel a strong attraction, and establish an intimate familiarity that allows them to broach the subject of violent fantasies. Tacit or vocalized approval from one to the other encourages acting out, and if the partners succeed together in committing a violent crime without getting caught, they feel both justified and eager to do it again. The dominant person is generally charismatic and maintains psychological control: his or her ideas and preferences set the tone. From post-arrest reports, team members indicate that they sensed the potential for partnership soon after meeting. Either they felt a strong romantic attraction or they had established a working familiarity.

With weak or nonexistent moral boundaries, they work together to expand their range of criminal creativity, but they often don't last. Generally they fall apart, because one turns on the other.

In the case of Graham and Wood, regardless of who actually performed the murders, their fantasies and activities enhanced their sadomasochistic sex. Thus, until they broke up, the so-called game became an essential aspect of their pleasure and a way for each to manipulate the other. They egged each other on, but they also exploited the fear of discovery to threaten each other. That killing elderly women also gave them an outlet for issues they both had with their mothers added yet another level of shared motivation. All in all, they found murder to be both fun and satisfying, and it bonded them together, so they kept going.

Given the range of human behavior and motivation, we haven't exhausted all the reasons why an HCSK might kill, but our list of motives does provide a way to collect the types of traits and behaviors revealed by those HCSKs who have been arrested and convicted. As such, we can assist those who work with them to know what to look for, as well as provide ideas for healthcare facilities to change the conditions that assist their clandestine and fatal activities.

10

Red Flags and Reform

COLLECTING THE FLAGS

Dr. Gregory Moffatt, a therapist and expert in risk assessment, examines murders that occur where they are not expected. He believes there are specific predictors of a predisposition toward violence that are generally overlooked by people acquainted with a killer. There is a way to identify the person who may become violent, he argues, and offers a list of warnings to take seriously. While he does not directly address the population of nurses and physicians who may become killers, his warning signs are nevertheless applicable.

Among the signals for potential violence are a past history of violence, actual threats made, continuous social isolation, substance abuse, employment instability, poor self-image, anger or depression, severe situational stress, having little to no support system, and a feeling of having been wronged.[1]

This list is helpful, but most HCSKs have no prior criminal background and often make no threats. However, other indicators are often found on lists of risk factors for HCSKs. More of these killers have been convicted in the past 15 years than in decades before, so it's clear we're either catching a higher percentage of them or more of them are developing. In either case, hospitals must acknowledge their existence and train their personnel to spot them, document their movements, and take action, both before and after crimes occur. In retrospect, it always looks easier to have noticed and caught a HCSK than it actually was, and that opens the door to nit-picking armchair detectives. Yet as mentioned before, prospective profiling, or viewing crime via a blueprint has its problems as well, but becoming aware of the collection of red flags common to these killers can assist the colleagues and supervisors of an HCSK in spotting him or her more quickly.

Several professionals have collected the cases worldwide and made lists of traits and behaviors that should be taken seriously. Paula Lampe suggests that those nurses who seem compulsive, secretive, and consistently in the area of emergencies or code blues ought to be the focus of more scrutiny.[2] British physician and toxicologist Robert Forrest, involved with several cases in England, lists the many types of substances these HCSKs use, as well as victim characteristics and predatory behaviors,[3] while Dr. Vincent Marks, professor emeritus of clinical biochemistry in Britain, focuses specifically on killers injecting insulin.[4] Lucy and Aitken from Scotland have written about the use of statistical evidence to document an HCSK's presence during fatal medical emergencies,[5] and Karl Beine in Germany offered one of the first scientific studies in 2003,[6] followed up by a more comprehensive examination three years later by Yorker and others of 45 international cases since 1970.[7] Others have written about the phenomenon of HCSKs in true crime books devoted to specific cases. Thanks to these researchers, we can offer a fairly comprehensive list.

The Yorker, et al. study collected 147 cases from 20 countries of healthcare professionals charged with murder (not all were serial killers or victimizing patients), reviewed 90 prosecutions (some cases are pending and some resulted in acquittals), and listed brief details of 45 cases in which a practitioner was found guilty of serial murder (five had pled guilty to lesser charges and others were convicted of attempted murders). For eight, there proved to be insufficient evidence to convict. Collectively, they were thought to be responsible for over 2,000 patient deaths, although they were successfully prosecuted in just over 300 cases. Several had used more than one method to kill and quite a few suffered from a diagnosable mental disorder. Yet there were also sadists among this group, and outright psychopaths.

There are signals pointing to a specific suspect that have come up during a number of these cases, and those on the following list should be taken quite seriously:

• Statistically, there is a higher death rate when the suspected person is on shift.

• A number of deaths in a cluster were unexpected.

• The death symptoms were also not expected, given the patient's illness or procedure.

• Patients or their families have complained about the person's treatment of the patient.

• The suspect has been given macabre nicknames by patients or others on staff, such as "Death Angel," "Killer Joe," "The Terminator," "and "Dr. Death."

- The suspect was seen entering rooms where deaths occurred, especially rooms of patients not assigned to that person.
- Unexpected substances are associated with the death.

The next list is a comprehensive checklist of personality traits and behaviors that have been associated with HCSKs. Although none of these items is in itself sufficient to place someone under a cloud of suspicion, a number of them together in constellation should be alarming to the person's colleagues and supervisors, as well as to the facility administrators. Among the red flags for spotting HCSKs are that the suspected person:

- has moved around from one facility to another
- is secretive or has a difficult time with personal relationships
- has a history of mental instability or periodic depression
- likes to predict when someone will die
- makes odd comments or jokes about killing patients or being jinxed
- likes to talk about death with colleagues or shows odd behaviors related to the death (excitement, ownership, undue curiosity, strange fantasies)
- has a higher incidence of code blues or deaths on his or her shift
- seems inordinately enthused about his or her skills, and likes to arrive early or stay late on a shift
- has made inconsistent statements when asked about incidences
- keeps to him- or herself and prefers shifts where fewer colleagues and supervisors are around (generally the night shift)
- is associated with several incidents at different institutions
- has been involved with other criminal activities
- makes colleagues anxious or suspicious
- seems to crave attention
- tries to prevent others from checking on patients
- hangs around during the immediate death investigation
- is in possession of suspect substances in his or her home, locker, or personal effects
- has been found to have lied about personal information or credentials, or falsified reports
- is in possession of books about poison or serial murder
- has had disciplinary problems
- appears to have a personality disorder
- has a substance abuse problem

Identifying such people as soon as possible requires documenting patterns of behavior and finding physical evidence that links the suspected individual to the crimes. Unfortunately, intentional killers, as well as people who become addicted to killing as the result of a mercy killing or two, have the perfect arena in which to get away with murder for long periods of time. Hospitals are places of trust and the means to kill patients are readily available. In addition, medical murders are not easily detected. Stopping this phenomenon requires a sharp eye, an awareness that any care facility is vulnerable, and a desire to ensure that suspicious people be taken seriously.

Let's see what an expert has to say, then examine the conditions in healthcare facilities that may actually assist these killers, as well as ways to decrease their numbers and minimize or even stop their activities.

AN EXPERT'S PERSPECTIVE

Beatrice Crofts Yorker, described earlier as one of the first researchers in this area, has studied HCSKs for two decades. She's in a good position, then, to notice trends. "In terms of what we've seen recently," she says, "there have been more cases in Europe, while it's been flattening in the United States. They have either become more devious or people are more reluctant to report and prosecute because it is so onerous. In high-tech areas, particularly the United States, there are more safeguards. For example, they are monitoring non-controlled drugs much better now—mostly for cost containment, but it has the side effect of possibly deterring or making this activity a little less invisible.

"The high-tech healthcare environment almost invites sociopaths to do this. Sociopaths are represented in all occupations, in all economic strata. It is too easy to kill a patient when you don't even have to stick their skin with a needle. You simply put a needle in their IV line with ordinary, soluble, everyday medication. You just need to put in a ml or two more. The brink between toxic and therapeutic doses of what are usually therapeutic medications is so imperceptible."

Aside from the motives stated in the previous chapter, she has noticed another:

There is this whole issue of "healing myself." Isn't it interesting that among the clergy we have repressed sexual deviants who were drawn to the clergy because they were thinking, "maybe if I'm in this field it will help me control this." We also have unhappy people who go into psychiatry or psychology because they think if they learn how to heal, maybe it will work on them. People go into the healthcare field sometimes because they are drawn to medical crises. I am well aware that we may have more of our share of formerly abused children among those in the healthcare field and I'm not sure if it is just the demographics these days of women and girls who are abused, but they find themselves going into nursing and a lot of them are engaged in trauma repetition compulsion—if I can have control, then I'm the one in charge of hurting people or not hurting people. The healing field is a source of power, so this is no surprise to me as a nursing educator. We see a fair amount of nursing students who have character disorders, although it's only the extremely rare case that we would want to exclude from the profession because they might kill patients. You can't tell. We can't do screening for predictive traits at this time. But that might change.[8]

FACILITATING MURDER

No hospital, nursing home, or other healthcare facility would knowingly assist a practitioner to kill patients, but the nature of healthcare and the constant demands on the system inadvertently provide an easy avenue for predators. Among the most pronounced conditions are:

- Disbelief and/or denial that an HCSK might be operating in the facility
- Lack of cooperation from administrators for law enforcement or research
- Murder weapons that are difficult to detect
- The easy availability of medications that can be fatal in certain doses
- The need for complex statistical analysis and the tracking of cases
- Lesser supervision on some shifts
- Lack of training in the dangerous nature of certain personality disorders
- Lack of training in evidence preservation
- Punishment for whistle-blowers
- The situation of "floating," in which nurses move from one hospital area to another and are not easily held to account for specific patients
- The superficial nature of background checks
- Reluctance to give poor performance evaluations or withhold recommendations, for fear of lawsuits
- Lack of central reporting databases for nurses

We need to deal with these cases in a pre-emptive fashion, not after the fact, and we can. But to do so means erasing some of the institutional self-protective devices that have given these people shelter and assistance. Admitting that medical institutions are vulnerable to the invasion, and even the making, of a predator is a fact; only if we accept that fact and work to change it will we ensure that we make HCSKs either less effective in the future or less likely to exploit the medical system.

MAKING CHANGES

Carol N. Dunbar, writing in *Forensic Nurse,* points to the way physician data is compiled in two systems, the National Practitioner Database (NPDB) and the Federation of State Medical Boards (FSMB). In the latter, state boards compile reports about disciplinary action, malpractice, and any hospital sanctions of physicians. Thus, problems can be monitored and other facilities made aware of them. She believes that there should be similar centralized systems for other healthcare practitioners, noting that the National Council of State Boards of Nursing (NCSBN) is attempting to achieve this, via the Nursys Data Bank. However, only 27 boards participate, which limits the amount of data that facilities have access to. And there's no guarantee that a suspicious practitioner will even be reported.[9]

Yorker, too, has advice for healthcare agencies. "They should check on the veracity or truthfulness of their applicants and ask them regular ordinary questions, like marital status or where they went to school, or their license plate number, and then really check credentials. They should check the items that are most easy to verify through public records and get the applicant's permission to verify things. If any of that verifiable information indicates that they are lying, that is a much bigger red flag than is having a criminal background. Of course, people will lie for a lot of reasons and it doesn't mean they are going to kill patients, but of our 90 prosecutions, falsifying credentials was prevalent and only a couple had criminal backgrounds. But nurse after nurse who was accused of murder had multiple incidents of fabrications and falsification.

"Also, call the last three places of employment and ask if the applicant was associated with any increase in adverse patient outcomes or patient incidents. And the prior hospital or facility should truthfully answer. The policy has been to give out only dates of employment and not to say anything that is potentially damaging because of fear of liability. I'm saying, get over that. At worst that would be $35,000 if it was proven that [the facility] was deliberately lying about that nurse's reputation. Compare that to eight million dollars from wrongful death lawsuits."[10]

It's important to include nurses on staff who are trained in evidence handling and documentation, and thus have a better eye for this sinister behavior than most other healthcare workers. They would understand the significance of a spike in the mortality rate, a cluster of unexpected deaths, a nurse's unusual behavior, and a shortage of certain types of medication.

Everything is potential evidence. One never knows what small thing might be important to a later investigation. Even non-physical items, such as a person discussing a violent fantasy, can have evidentiary value. Education about these killers is the best way to erode denial and naiveté, perhaps the killers' most effective allies in the medical system.

HEALTHCARE STRATEGIES FOR PREVENTION

1. Although it seems ironic that serial killers in the healthcare system might have advice to offer as to how to stop them, who knows better than they how the system can be exploited? For example, in a spirit of cooperation, both Cullen and Harvey gave extensive interviews as to how they operated and what was wrong at the facilities where they worked. Their accusatory views were probably exaggerated to some extent, because predators often like to assign blame, but doing more interviews with HCSKs, similar to what the FBI did during the 1980s with incarcerated killers, would be a good start. That task would be in the hands of investigators working in cooperation with healthcare facilities.

2. Educate workers at all responsible levels as to what to look for in terms of behavioral red flags and make a complaint-friendly environment among supervisors

3. Do a thorough background check of new hires, and don't be persuaded by the lack of a criminal record. Nurse recruitment in times of nursing shortages can sometimes become lax, allowing unqualified personnel to be hired. Most known HCSKs had never had a criminal record.

4. Work toward changing laws that punish institutions that pass along poor behavioral reviews of problem employees.

5. Have someone on staff, such as a forensic nurse, who has training in forensic investigation. They can liaison with police, informing them about who may have handled potential evidence, and can attend any necessary court appearances. In addition, forensic nurses can coach potential witnesses in courtroom protocol.

6. Clearly communicate "do not rehire" information to hospitals checking on a prior employee.

7. In the event of a suspicious cluster of deaths, get law enforcement involved. Also consult with other hospitals that have had such an investigation.

8. Do the investigation quietly, so as not to alert the suspect.

9. Institute better pharmacy accounting of drugs used, especially those that can be lethal.

10. Even with computerized systems, do periodic drug use and data reviews.

11. Institute psychiatric assessment as part of the hiring process.

12. Institute documentation and tracking of all deaths and illnesses.

Thirty-eight states have adopted laws protecting the employers, and some protect the discussion of job performance and reasons for termination, unless a person who decides to sue can show evidence that is clear and convincing of reckless disclosure of false information or malicious intent on the part of the employer. Risk managers should become familiar with the requirements of their state for obtaining needed background checks. They are also expected to know about adjoining jurisdictions, because employees may be drawn from bordering states.

Forensic nurse Dana DeVito has written about this issue. She states that professional nursing agencies such as the New Jersey State Nurses Association (NJSNA) and the American Nurses Association (ANA) agree that the public's trust in the nursing profession is greatly eroded when a nurse intentionally harms a patient. Both agencies believe that safeguards for the public require that a healthcare agency should be self-reporting, similar to the procedures for the mandatory reporting of suspected child abuse cases. Suspicious activities, as well as data about frequent terminations, patient overdoses, high cardiac arrest or high rates of death associated with an individual nurse, could be reported and collected in a national data bank. This would provide a coordinated and accessible method for monitoring dangerous nursing professionals.[11]

When the Cullen case broke, U.S. Senators Jon S. Corzine and Frank R. Lautenberg from New Jersey issued a statement: "The confessed killing spree ripped open shocking flaws in the nation's system of screening healthcare professionals."[12] They were among the first to call for shake-up and reform. As such, they have spearheaded legislation aimed at creating mandatory hospital reporting requirements. Unveiled in 2004, this legislation was called the Safe Healthcare Reporting Act, or SHARE Act, and required that any adverse employment action against a healthcare professional related to professional conduct or competence be reported to both professional licensing boards and the National Practitioner Databank.

With legislation pending, the healthcare facilities, together with legal departments and risk management, can develop internal pathways for reporting violations. Peer review systems and internal investigations would better protect and ensure patient safety.

Risk management and nurse educators in healthcare facilities can collaborate to craft written policies and procedures to provide standard pathways for the reporting of suspicious activities of fellow nurses. These departments, in conjunction with a forensically trained nurse, can then interpret this information to spot trends, such as a high incidence of deaths on a specific person's shift, which may help ensure the safety of all patients.

RESPONSES

When an investigation turned up Saldivar in California, the Glendale Adventist Medical Center put out a statement, apologizing to families and assuring them they were helping the police. The hospital spokesperson said that they had no idea how Saldivar obtained the drugs that he used, but as a result of this case they had tightened their own controls and procedures. Hereafter, they would

1. institute a "mortality analysis," in which a single physician would review all records after a death, thus making it possible to spot suspicious trends and patterns;

2. have greater controls over the types of drugs that could be used to induce death;

3. subject all respiratory technicians to the orders of a physician for the use of a ventilator;

4. utilize computer surveillance of all ventilator settings, so that changes made would be recorded on a printed report; and

5. ensure that any medications not used during a code blue resuscitation would be secured at the conclusion of the incident.

Apparently, there's nothing like a serial killer prowling hospital corridors to make those in charge rethink their procedures. It's not that they were reluctant to make a change; it's that they believed procedures were sufficient and they had been shocked into realizing otherwise.

In Britain, after Shipman's conviction, the pharmacists who dispensed drugs to him came under investigation, but were cleared of misconduct. Nevertheless, tighter procedures have been proposed for controlling drug dispensing, as an amendment to the Misuse of Drugs Regulation Act of 2001. The proposal includes a way to make information available about all prescriptions from a single prescriber, and all healthcare providers would be required to make an annual declaration about the drugs they have on their premises. Pharmacists, too, must gather more personal information before filling a prescription.

In addition, the activities of doctors have come into tighter regulations, scaring some of them into becoming more conservative with pain medications. The movement is on to remove their right to self-vet and the General Medical Council is set to be stripped of its powers to discipline. In addition, coroners gained new powers to get organizations where deaths have occurred to respond to their reports and to devise reforms, if necessary, for which they will be held accountable. A chief coroner will keep track of these reports and monitor responses. Some say these reforms are still not sufficient and they call for stricter supervision for certifying doctors, as well as some way to ensure that deaths in need of investigation will in fact be properly reported.

In New Zealand, the Medical Council instituted pro-active audits designed to catch doctors engaging in misconduct. Although it is expected to take a decade to audit them all, the process is already in place. Questionnaires are completed by 16 of each doctor's professional colleagues and paramedical colleagues, as well as 10 randomly selected patients.

Stephan Letter's killings forced the clinic where he worked to review and revise its procedures, because the stolen drugs should not have been so easily accessible. Yet no one apparently noticed that someone was pilfering significant amounts across a period of time until many people were dead. The German Hospice Foundation called for Germany to introduce uniform checks, with medically qualified coroners viewing every patient who died in hospitals and homes for the elderly.

In countries where technology is developed, the move is afoot to computerize all medications, even allowing patients access to their records to check for themselves what they're being given. They can use the system to communicate with their doctors as well, asking questions and ensuring that they have their medical records ready to hand. This will also provide ways of tracking medication in situations of abuse, and of keeping tighter control.

With incidences of HCSKs increasing, rare as they may still be, hiring institutions in the healthcare professions have a duty to screen employees for potential predators. A proactive approach needs to be developed instead of waiting for legislative mandates. Written policies and procedures for reporting suspicious activities, accurate documentation, and cogent coordination of all the data collected, along with protection for those who do report, should all be considered. With the cooperation and input of the legal, nursing, and risk management departments, red flags may appear sooner, and could be addressed, thus potentially avoiding patient injuries and deaths.

THE TRUTH ABOUT PREDATORS

There is no way to predict a specific type of behavior, which may show us novelties at any time, but we can learn from past cases what kinds of behaviors are common to these incidents and thus detect similar cases in the future. Yet the healthcare system must cooperate. Numerous physicians and nurses have been inadvertently protected by administrators, and thus their compulsion to harm or kill continued.

It is unfortunately a fact of bureaucracy that in order to retain customers administrators might be tempted to hide whatever sheds a negative light on their facility, but since the paramount issue with hospitals is customer trust, effective attention to the problem of HCSKs actually assists that goal. The fact that a facility has detected and stopped a predator is in its favor—especially in light of the embarrassment it will suffer if a successive facility accomplishes it and then asks why they weren't told about this person. Protecting a predator, even with nothing more than passive avoidance, actually makes a facility appear to be *less* safe for patients. Quick-fix Band-Aids are generally insufficient to treat a deeply-rooted injury.

While one bad employee doesn't make an entire facility unsafe or medical practice generally corrupt, media-assisted public perception can exaggerate the situation. Yet by that same token, a healthcare facility can utilize the media to improve the image. Somerset County Medical Center, in the Cullen case, came out looking like both the victim of other institutions and society's hero for putting an end to Cullen's 16-year spate of patient termination.

No system is foolproof, and clever predators who really want to find a way around it, will. However, the more challenging and intimidating the hindrances and safeguards, the more likely that some potential killers will either keep their fantasies to themselves or turn their aggression toward some other venue—hopefully one in which victims are not quite as vulnerable and can more easily resist, identify, or elude them. It's not possible to fully protect the healthcare system from serial killers, but knowledge about their motives and methods will offer a better defense.

Notes

INTRODUCTION

1. Beatrice C. Yorker, Kenneth Kizer, Paula Lampe, Robert Forrest, et al., "Serial Murder by Healthcare Professionals," *Journal of Forensic Science,* 2006, Vol. 51, No. 6, p. 1362.

2. Ibid., p. 4.

3. Kelly Pyrek, "Healthcare Serial Killers: Recognizing the Red Flags," *Forensic Nurse,* September/October 2003, p. 1.

4. Jan Velinger, "Nurse committed murders to 'test' doctors," http://www.radio.cz/en/article/85964, May 15, 2006; "Czech Serial Killer May Have Murdered Five More Patients," *The Prague Daily Monitor,* January 25, 2007.

CHAPTER 1

1. John Camp, *One Hundred Years of Medical Murders* (London: Grafton Books, 1982), pp. 140–155.

2. Filsen Young, ed., *The Trial of Hawley Harvey Crippen* (London: W. Hodge, 1920).

3. Lecture delivered by Isadore Mihalikis, Bethlehem, PA, January 2003.

4. Joe McGinnis, *Fatal Vision* (New York: Random House, 1985); J. A. Potter and Fred Bost, *Fatal Justice: Reinvestigating the MacDonald Murders* (New York: W. W. Norton, 1995).

5. Kathleen Johnston, "Staff at New Orleans Hospital Debated Euthanizing Patients," CNN.com. October 13, 2005; Caroline Graham and Jo Knowsley, "We Had to Kill Our Patients," *The Daily Mail,* September 11, 2005. Retrieved January 11, 2007.

6. D. Asch and M. DeKay, "Euthanasia among Critical Care Nurses: Practices, Attitudes, and Social and Professional Correlates," *Medical Care* (35), September 1997, pp. 890–900.

7. Matt Bean, "Mallard Hit Hard with Fifty Years," CourtTV.com, July 1, 2003.

8. Jim Irwin, "Man Gets Life in 1969 Slaying," *The Detroit News,* September 1, 2005.

CHAPTER 2

1. John Camp, *One Hundred Years of Medical Murder* (London: Triad Grafton Books, 1982), pp. 7–32.

2. Ibid., pp. 95–113.

3. Harold Schecter, *Depraved* (New York: Pocket Books, 1998).

4. Kenneth V. Iserson, *Demon Doctors* (Tucson, AZ: Galen Press, 2002), pp. 133–162; Gregg Olson, *Starvation Heights* (New York: Warner, 1997).

5. John Camp, *One Hundred Years of Medical Murder* (London: Triad Grafton Books, 1982), pp. 156–175; Kenneth v. Iserson, *Demon Doctors* (Tucson, AZ: Galen Press, 2002), pp. 207–262.

6. Robert Jay Lifton, *The Nazi Doctors* (New York: Basic Books, 1986), pp. 337–83.

7. Harold Schechter, *Fatal* (New York: Pocket Books, 2004).

8. "Official Report of the Trial of Sarah Jane Robinson for the Murder of Prince Arthur Freeman, in the Supreme Judicial Court of Massachusetts, from the Notes of Mr. J.M.W. Yerrington" (Boston: Wright & Potter, 1888).

9. Michael D. Kelleher and C. L. Kelleher, *Murder Most Rare: The Female Serial Killer* (New York: Dell, 1998), pp. 138–140.

10. Ibid., pp. 201–203.

CHAPTER 3

1. "Death Follows Art," *Time,* March 22, 1976; "Dr. X Indicted," *Time,* May 31, 1976; "A Jury Sets Dr. X Free," *Time,* November 6, 1978.

2. J. B. Stewart, *Blind Eye: How the Medical Establishment Let a Doctor Get Away with Murder* (New York: Simon & Schuster, 1999), p. 95.

3. *U.S. vs. Michael J. Swango,* No. 99R00496 (U.S. filed July 11, 2000); Sara Bean, "SIU Med School Graduate Charged in Killing Five Zimbabwe Patients," *Daily Egyptian,* January 28, 1998; Linda Prager, "Former Resident Swango Pleads Guilty to Killing Three Patients," Amednews.com, October 2, 2000.

4. J. B. Stewart, *Blind Eye: How the Medical Establishment Let a Doctor Get Away with Murder* (New York: Simon & Schuster, 1999), p. 95.

5. R. Horton, "The Real Lessons from Harold Frederick Shipman, *Lancet,* January 13, 2001, 357 (9250), pp. 82–83; Brian Whittle and Jean Ritchie, *Harold Shipman: Prescription for Murder* (London: Warner, 2000); "The Death that Led Shipman to the Dock," *BBC News,* January 31, 2000.

6. John Surtees, *The Strange Case of Dr. Bodkins Adams, and the Views of Those Who Knew Him* (London: SB Publications, 2000).

7. Terry Ganey, "Convicted Killer Glennon Engleman Dies at 71; City Dentist Killed for Money," *St. Louis Post Dispatch,* March 4, 1999.

8. Brian Bromberger and Janet Fife-Yeomans, *Deep Sleep: Harry Bailey and the Scandal of Chelmsford* (East Roseville, New South Wales: Simon & Schuster-Australia, 1991); D. Gareth Jones, "Contemporary Medical Scandals: A Challenge to Ethical Codes and Ethical Principles," *Perspectives on Science and Christian Faith,* No. 42, March 1990, pp. 2–14.

CHAPTER 4

1. Richard Glynn Jones. *Poison!* (Secaucus, NJ: Lyle Stuart, Inc., 1987); Carey Goldberg, "Former Nurse on Trial in Patients' Deaths," *The New York Times,* November 23, 2000.

2. Terry Manner, *Deadlier than the Male: Stories of Female Serial Killers* (London: Pan Books, 1995), pp. 254–291.

3. Marc D. Feldman, Charles V. Ford, and Toni Reinhold, *Patient or Pretender: Inside the Strange World of Factitious Disorders* (New York: John Wiley, 1994), pp. 13–16.

4. Richard Asher, "Munchausen Syndrome," *Lancet,* 1951, 1: 339–341; R. J. McClure, P. M. Davis, S. R. Meadow, and J. R. Silbert. "Epidemiology of Munchausen Syndrome by Proxy, Non-accidental Poisoning and Non-accidental Suffocation," *Archive of Diseases in Children,* 1996, 75, pp. 57–61.

5. Deborah Schurman-Kauflin, *The New Predator: Profiles of Female Serial Killers* (New York: Algora, 2000), p. 37.

6. Peter Elkind, *The Death Shift: The True Story of Nurse Genene Jones and the Texas Baby Murders* (New York: Viking, 1983).

7. Michael D. Kelleher and C. L. Kelleher, *Murder Most Rare: The Female Serial Killer* (New York: Dell, 1998), pp. 240–246; Michael Newton, *The Encyclopedia of Serial Killers,* 2nd ed. (New York: Checkmark Books, 2006), p. 254.

8. Angela K. Brown, "Texas Nurse Gets Life in 10 Deaths," October 5, 2006. www.sfgate.com, retrieved January 23, 2007; "Nurse Indicted on Additional Counts in Texas Hospital Deaths," www.kron4.com, 2004.

9. From an interview with Beatrice Yorker, January 10, 2007.

10. "French Nurse Jailed in Six Deaths," *The New York Times,* February 1, 2003.

11. "Nurse Accused of Killing 13 Patients Insists She's Innocent as Trial Nears," Canada.com, September 24, 2002.

12. Richard D. Gill, "Nurse Lucia de B Convicted of Serial Murder by Every Statistical Mistake in the Book," www.math.leidenuniv.nl, retrieved December 20, 2006.

13. Paula Lampe, *The Mother Teresa Syndrome,* (Holland: Nelissen, 2002), p 3.

14. Ibid., pp. 28–54.

15. Michael Newton, *The Encyclopedia of Serial Killers*, 2nd ed. (New York: Checkmark Books, 2006), p. 241.

16. Brian Lane and Wilfred Gregg. *The Encyclopedia of Serial Killers* (New York: Berkeley, 1995), pp. 31–32.

CHAPTER 5

1. Kelly Pyrek. "Healthcare Serial Killers: Recognizing the Red Flags," *Forensic Nurse,* September/October 2003.

2. Jack Goulding, "12 Victims for the Angel of Death," in *Medical Murders,* edited by Rose G. Mandelsberg (New York: Pinnacle Books, 1992), pp. 194–206. *People v. Richard Angelo,* 88 N.Y. 2d 217 666 N.E. 2d 1333, 644 N.Y.S. 2d 460 (1996).

3. "Defendant tells of One Night in the Hospital Ward," *The New York Times,* November 20, 1987.

4. Philip Gutis, "Slaying Inquiry Builds against L. I. Nurse," *The New York Times,* November 18, 1987.

5. "Closing Arguments in Majors' Murder Trial Portray Former Nurse as God and Scapegoat," *Court TV Online,* October 13, 1999; *Indiana v. Orville Lynn Majors,* Probable Cause Affidavit.

6. Andrew Buncombe, "Nurse Is Guilty of Killing with Drug-rape Drink," London *The Independent,* May 18, 2000.

7. Beatrice Crofts Yorker, Kenneth W. Kizer, Paula Lampe, R. Forrest, Jacquetta M. Lannan, Donna A. Russell, "Serial Murder by Healthcare Professionals" *Journal of Forensic Sciences* 51, 2006 (6), 1362–1371.

8. Tim Larimer, "Very Questionable Care," TimeAsia.com, Vol. 157, No. 3, January 22, 2001.

9. Transcript of the interview with Charles Cullen from the *Newark Star-Ledger.*

10. Scott Kraus, "Seven Nurses had Warned about Killer," *The Morning Call,* July 10, 2005.

11. "In His Own Words," *The Newark Star Ledger,* September 12, 2004.

12. Max Alexander, "Killer on Call," *Reader's Digest.* November 2004; "Angel of Death," A&E, Special Reports, Feb 2004. Rick Hepp, "Killer Nurse Blasts Judge for Unsealing Violent Past," *The Star Ledger,* June 10, 2006. Scott Kraus, "Cullen Admits Murders, Is Spared the Death Penalty," *The Morning Call,* April 30, 2004.

13. Stewart Payne. "A&E Nurse poisoned 18 Patients so he Could Enjoy Trying to Save Them," *Telegraph Group,* February 15, 2006; "Killer Nurse Addicted to Thrills," BBC News, April 18, 2006.

14. "Swiss Nurse Is Sentenced for 22 Murders," *The New York Times,* January 29, 2005.

15. Tony Patterson, "Stephan Letter Wanted to 'Help' Patients," *The Independent,* February 8, 2006; "German Male Nurse Admits Killings," *BBC News,* February 7, 2006.

CHAPTER 6

1. Michael Palmer, *The Sisterhood* (New York: Bantam, 1990).
2. F. Protzman, "Killing of 49 patients by 4 nurse's aids stuns the Austrians," *The New York Times,* April 18, 1989.
3. L. Cauffiel, *Forever and Five Days* (New York: Zebra Books, 1992); "Women Killed to Assure Love, One Testifies," *Detroit Free Press,* September 14, 1989.
4. William Whalen, *Defending Donald Harvey* (Cincinnati, Ohio: Emmis Books, 2005).
5. Barbara Geehr, "Murdering Angel of Mercy," *Medical Murders,* edited by Rose G. Mandelsberg (New York: Pinnacle Books, 1992), pp. 69–86.
6. Brian Lane and Wilfred Gregg. *The Encyclopedia of Serial Killers* (New York: Berkeley, 1995), pp. 275–26.
7. "Statement Regarding Arrest of Former Employee," by Mark Newmyer, Glendale Adventist Medical Center, January 10, 2002.
8. Paul Lieberman, "Graveyard Shift," *The Los Angeles Times,* April 25, 2002; "Saldivar Sentenced to Six Consecutive Sentences of Life without Parole," District Attorney County of Los Angeles Media Relations News Release, March 2002; "LA Angel of Death Sentenced to Life," *Washington Post,* Thursday, April 18, 2002.
9. Brian Lane and Wilfred Gregg, *The Encyclopedia of Serial Killers* (New York: Berkeley, 1995), pp. 29–31.
10. "Indonesian Sorcerer Sentenced to Death," *BBC News,* April 14, 1998.

CHAPTER 7

1. Tim O'Leary, "Former Nurse Admits to Serial Killings; Avoids Risk of Death Penalty," *The Press Enterprise,* September 10, 1998; "Judge Orders Life Terms for Murders," *The Press Enterprise,* October 17, 1998.
2. Kenneth Iserson, *Demon Doctors: Physicians as Serial Killers* (Tucson, Arizona: Galen Press, 2002), pp. 305–311.
3. "Judge Rules Gay Prey Serial Killer Richard Rogers Jury Will Hear Similar Slayings," Queerday.com, Sept. 29, 2005; Osborn, Duncan, "An Accused Serial Killer on Trial," *Gay City News,* Volume 3, January 29–February 4, 2004; Wayne Parry, "Trial of Richard Rogers to Hear about Slayings, Dismemberment of Four Gay, Bisexual men," *Associated Press,* ABCNews.go.com, Oct. 15, 2005; Damien Cave, "As Killer Faces Sentencing, His Motive Remains Elusive," *The New York Times,* January 27, 2006.
4. Catherine Wessinger, *How the Millennium Comes Violently* (New York: Seven Bridges Press, 2000), p. 135; Robert Jay Lifton, *Destroying the World to Save It: Aum Shinrikyo, Apocalyptic Violence and the New Global Terrorism* (New York: Henry Holt, 1999); "Conversation with Robert Jay Lifton," Institute of International Studies, globetrotter.berkley.edu, November 2, 1999.

CHAPTER 8

1. Darcy O'Brien, *The Hillside Stranglers* (New York: Carroll and Graf, 2003).

2. Ludovic Kennedy, *Ten Rillington Place* (New York: Simon & Schuster, 1961).

3. *State of Connecticut v. Amy E. Archer Gilligan;* M. William Phelps, "Entrepreneur, Caretaker, Serial Killer," media-server.amazon.com. Retrieved March 16, 2006; "Mrs. Gilligan Says She Is Persecuted," *The New York Times,* May 11, 1916.

4. Michael Kelleher and C. L. Kelleher, *Murder Most Rare: The Female Serial Killer* (New York: Dell, 1998), pp. 136–38.

5. "Bogus Doctor Gets 15-Year Imprisonment," English.people.com.cn, October 1, 2000.

CHAPTER 9

1. Carol Anne Davis, *Women Who Kill: Profiles of Female Serial Killers* (Great Britain: Allison and Busby, Ltd., 2001), pp. 122–124.

2. Eric Fromm, *The Anatomy of Human Destructiveness* (New York: Owl Books, 1992). pp. 362–367.

3. Katherine Ramsland, *The Human Predator: A Historical Chronicle of Serial Murder and Forensic Investigation* (New York: Berkley, 2005), pp. 282–283.

4. "Why Some Doctors Kill," Broadcast, *The Health Report,* Robert Kaplan with Norman Swan, July 29, 2002. www.abc.net.au.

5. Robert Jay Lifton, *The Nazi Doctors* (New York: Basic Books, 1986), pp. 418–465.

6. Al C. Carlisle, "The Dark Side of the Serial-Killer Personality," in *Serial Killers,* edited by Louis Gerdes (San Diego, CA: Greenhaven Press, 2000), p. 107; excerpted from "The Divided Self: Toward an Understanding of the Dark Side of the Serial Killer," *American Journal of Criminal Justice,* Vol. 17, no. 2, 1993.

CHAPTER 10

1. Gregory Moffatt, *Blind-Sided: Homicide Where It Is Least Expected* (Westport, Connecticut: Praeger, 2000), pp. 163–184.

2. Paula Lampe, *The Mother Teresa Syndrome* (Holland: Nelissen, 2002); *Angels of Death* (Holland: Nelissen, 2007).

3. Robert Forrest, "Serial Homicide by Health Care Professionals," Presentation at the American Academy of Forensic Sciences conference, San Antonio, Texas, February 22, 2007.

4. Vincent Marks, with Caroline Richmond, *Insulin Killers* (London: RSM Press, 2007).

5. David Lucy and Colin Aitken, "A Review of the Role of Roster Data and Evidence of Attendance in Cases of Suspected Excess Deaths in a Medical Context," *Law, Probability and Risk* (2002) 1, pp. 141–160.

6. Karl H. Beine, "Homicides of Patients in Hospitals and Nursing Homes: A Comparative Analysis of Case Series," *International Journal of Law and Psychiatry,* 26 (2003), pp. 373–386.

7. Beatrice Crofts Yorker, Kenneth Kizer, Paula Lampe, Robert Forrest, et al., "Serial Murder by Healthcare Professionals," *Journal of Forensic Science,* November 2006, Vol. 51, No. 6, pp. 1362–1371.

8. Interview with Beatrice Yorker, January 10, 2007.

9. Carol N. Dunbar, "Nurses Who Kill: Picking up the Pieces after the Charles Cullen Arrest," *Forensic Nurse,* September 2005, pp. 1–2.

10. Interview with Beatrice Yorker, January 10, 2007.

11. Katherine Ramsland and Dana DeVito, "Nurses who Kill," *Nursing Malpractice,* 3rd ed. (Tucson, Arizona: Lawyers & Judges Publishing, 2007), p. 878.

12. Dunbar, ibid., p. 1.

Bibliography

"A Jury Sets Dr. X Free." *Time*, November 6, 1978.

Alexander, Max. "Killer on Call." *Reader's Digest*, November 2004.

Asch, D. and M. DeKay. "Euthanasia Among Critical Care Nurses: Practices, Attitudes, and Social and Professional Correlates," *Medical Care* (35) September 1997, 890–900.

Bean, Matt. "Mallard Hit Hard with Fifty Years." CourtTV.com, July 1, 2003.

Bean, Sara. "SIU Med School Graduate Charged in Killing Five Zimbabwe Patients." *Daily Egyptian,* January 28, 1998.

Beine, Karl H. "Homicides of Patients in Hospitals and Nursing Homes: A Comparative Analysis of Case Series." *International Journal of Law and Psychiatry* (26) 2003, 373–386.

"Bogus Doctor Gets 15-Year Imprisonment." English.people.com.cn, October 1, 2000.

Bromberger, Brian and Janet Fife-Yeomans. *Deep Sleep: Harry Bailey and the Scandal of Chelmsford.* East Roseville, New South Wales: Simon & Schuster-Australia, 1991.

Buncombe, Andrew. "Nurse Is Guilty of Killing with Drug-rape Drink." London: *The Independent,* May 18, 2000.

Camp, John. *One Hundred Years of Medical Murders.* London: Triad Grafton Books, 1982.

Carlisle, A. C. "The Dark Side of the Serial-Killer Personality," in *Serial Killers,* edited by Louis Gerdes, San Diego, CA: Greenhaven Press, 2000. Excerpted from "The Divided Self: Toward an Understanding of the Dark Side of the Serial Killer." *American Journal of Criminal Justice,* Vol. 17, no. 2, 1993.

Cauffiel, Lowell. *Forever and Five Days.* New York: Zebra Books, 1992.

Cave, D. "As Killer Faces Sentencing, His Motive Remains Elusive." *The New York Times*, January 27, 2006.

"Closing Arguments in Majors' Murder Trial Portray Former Nurse as God and Scapegoat." CourtTV.com, October 13, 1999.

"Conversation with Robert Jay Lifton." Institute of International Studies, globetrotter. berkley.edu. November 2, 1999.

Cullen, Tom. *The Mild Murderer.* Boston: Houghton Mifflin, 1977.

"Czech Serial Killer May Have Murdered Five More Patients." *The Prague Daily Monitor,* January 25, 2007.

Davies, N. *Murder on Ward Four.* London: Catto and Windus, 1993.

Davis, Carol Anne. *Women Who Kill: Profiles of Female Serial Killers.* Great Britain: Allison and Busby, Ltd., 2001.

"Death Follows Art." *Time,* March 22, 1976.

"Defendant Tells of One Night in the Hospital Ward." *The New York Times,* November 20, 1987.

Diagnostic and Statistical Manual of Mental Disorders—IV. Washington, DC: American Psychiatric Association, 1994.

"Dr. X Indicted." *Time,* May 31, 1976.

Dunbar, Carol N. "Nurses Who Kill: Picking up the Pieces after the Charles Cullen Arrest," *Forensic Nurse,* September 2005.

Elkind, Peter. *The Death Shift: The True Story of Nurse Genene Jones and the Texas Baby Murders.* New York: Viking, 1983.

Feldman, Marc D., Charles V. Ford, and Toni Reinhold, *Patient or Pretender: Inside the Strange World of Factitious Disorders.* New York: John Wiley, 1994.

Forrest, Robert. "Nurses Who Systematically Harm Their Patients." *Medical Law International,* 1 (4), 114–121.

———. "Serial Homicide by Health Care Professionals." Presentation at the American Academy of Forensic Sciences. San Antonio, Texas. February 22, 2007.

Fromm, Eric. *The Anatomy of Human Destructiveness.* New York: Owl Books, 1992.

Ganey, T. "Convicted Killer Glennon Engleman Dies at 71; City Dentist Killed for Money." *St. Louis Post Dispatch*, March 4, 1999.

Geehr, Barbara. "Murdering Angel of Mercy," *Medical Murders,* edited by Rose G. Mandelsberg. New York: Pinnacle Books, 1992, 69–86.

"German Male Nurse Admits Killings." *BBC News*, February 7, 2006.

Goldberg, Carey. "Former Nurse on Trial in Patients' Deaths," *The New York Times,* November 23, 2000.

Goulding, Jack. "12 Victims for the Angel of Death," in *Medical Murders*, edited by Rose G. Mandelsberg. New York: Pinnacle Books, 1992.

Graham, C., and J. Knowsley. "We Had to Kill Our Patients." *The Daily Mail,* September 11, 2005.

Gutis, P. "Slaying Inquiry Builds against L. I. Nurse," *The New York Times*, November 18, 1987.

Hepp, Rick. "Killer Nurse Blasts Judge for Unsealing Violent Past." *The Star Ledger,* June 10, 2006.

Horton, R. "The Real Lessons from Harold Frederick Shipman." *Lancet*, 357 (9250), 82–83.

Indiana v. Orville Lynn Majors, Jr., Probable Cause Affidavit, Cause no. 83c0 1–971 2 CF-0074, December 1997.

"Indonesian Sorcerer Sentenced to Death." *BBC News*, April 14, 1998.

"In His Own Words." *The Star Ledger*, September 12, 2004.

Irwin, J. "Man Gets Life in 1969 Slaying." *The Detroit News*, September 1, 2005.

Iserson, Kenneth V. *Demon Doctors*. Tucson, AZ: Galen Press, 2002.

Johnston, K. "Staff at New Orleans Hospital Debated Euthanizing Patients." CNN.com. October 13, 2005.

Jones, D. Gareth. "Contemporary Medical Scandals: A Challenge to Ethical Codes and Ethical Principles." *Perspectives on Science and Christian Faith,* 42 (March 1990), 2–14.

Jones, Richard Glynn. *Poison!* Secaucus, NJ: Lyle Stuart, Inc., 1987.

"Judge Orders Life Terms for Murders." *The Press Enterprise*, October 17, 1998.

"Judge Rules Gay Prey Serial Killer Richard Rogers Jury Will Hear Similar Slayings." Queerday.com. September. 29, 2005.

Kaplan, Robert, with Norman Swan. "Why Some Doctors Kill." Broadcast, *The Health Report*, July 29, 2002, www.abc.net.au.

Kelleher, Michael D. and C. L. Kelleher. *Murder Most Rare: The Female Serial Killer.* New York: Dell, 1998.

Kennedy, L. *Ten Rillington Place*. New York: Simon & Schuster, 1961.

"Killer Nurse Addicted to Thrills." *BBC News*, April 18, 2006.

Kraus, Scott. "Cullen Admits Murders, Is Spared the Death Penalty." *The Morning Call*, April 30, 2004.

———. "Seven Nurses had Warned about Killer." *The Morning Call*, July 10, 2005.

"LA Angel of Death Sentenced to Life." *Washington Post*, Thursday, April 18, 2002.

Lampe, Paula. *Angels of Death*. Holland: Nelissen, 2007.

———. *The Mother Teresa Syndrome*. Holland: Nelissen, 2002.

Lane, Brian and Wilfred Gregg. *The Encyclopedia of Serial Killers*. New York: Berkeley, 1995.

Larimer, T. "Very Questionable Care." TimeAsia.com. 157 (3), January 22, 2001.

Lieberman, Paul. "Graveyard Shift," *The Los Angeles Times,* April 25, 2002.

Lifton, Robert Jay. *Destroying the World to Save It: Aum Shinrikyo, Apocalyptic Violence and the New Global Terrorism*. New York: Henry Holt, 1999.

———. *The Nazi Doctors*. New York: Basic Books, 1986.

Linedecker, Clifford L. and William A. Burt. *Nurses Who Kill*. New York: Pinnacle, 1990.

Linedecker, Clifford L. and Zach T. Martin. *Death Angel*. New York: Pinnacle, 2005.

Lucy, David and Colin Aitken. "A Review of the Role of Roster Data and Evidence of Attendance in Cases of Suspected Excess Deaths in a Medical Context," *Law, Probability and Risk* (1) 2002, 141–160.

Mair, George. *Angel of Death.* New York: Chamberlain Brothers, 2004.

Manner, Terry. *Deadlier than the Male: Stories of Female Serial Killers.* London: Pan Books, 1995.

Marks, Vincent, with Carolyn Richmond. *Insulin Murders.* London: RSM Press, 2007.

McClure, R. J., P. M. Davis, S. R. Meadow, and J. R. Silbert. "Epidemiology of Munchausen Syndrome by Proxy, Non-accidental Poisoning and Non-accidental Suffocation." *Archive of Diseases in Children,* 1996, 75, 57–61.

McGinnis, Joe. *Fatal Vision.* New York: Random House, 1985.

Moffatt, Gregory. *Blind-sided: Homicide Where It Is Least Expected.* Westport, CT: Praeger, 2000.

"Mrs. Gilligan Says She Is Persecuted." *The New York Times,* May 11, 1916.

Newton, Michael. *The Encyclopedia of Serial Killers.* Second Edition. New York: Checkmark Books, 2006.

"Nurse Accused of Killing Patients says She's Innocent as Trial Begins." *Canadian Press,* September 24, 2002.

"Nurses in Missouri and Texas Charged with Killing Patients." *Reuters,* July 18, 2002.

O'Brien, Darcy. *The Hillside Stranglers.* New York: Carroll and Graf, 2003.

"Official Report of the Trial of Sarah Jane Robinson for the Murder of Prince Arthur Freeman, in the Supreme Judicial Court of Massachusetts, from the Notes of Mr. J.M.W. Yerrington." Boston: Wright & Potter, 1888.

O'Leary, T. "Former Nurse Admits to Serial Killings; Avoids Risk of Death Penalty." *The Press Enterprise,* September 10, 1998.

Olson, Gregg. *Starvation Heights.* New York: Warner, 1997.

Osborn, Duncan. "An Accused Serial Killer on Trial," *Gay City News* 3, January 29–February 4, 2004.

Palmer, Michael. *The Sisterhood.* New York: Bantam, 1990.

Parry, W. "Trial of Richard Rogers to Hear about Slayings, Dismemberment of Four Gay, Bisexual Men." ABCNews.go.com. October 15, 2005.

Patterson, T. "Stephan Letter Wanted to 'Help' Patients," *The Independent,* February 2006.

Payne, S. "A&E Nurse Poisoned 18 Patients so He Could Enjoy Trying to Save Them." *Telegraph Group,* February 15, 2006.

People v. Richard Angelo, 88 N.Y. 2d 217 666 N.E. 2d 1333, 644 N.Y.S. 2d 460 (1996).

Phelps, M. William. "Entrepreneur, Caretaker, Serial Killer," media-server.amazon.com. Retrieved March 16, 2006.

Potter, J. A. and Fred Bost. *Fatal Justice: Reinvestigating the MacDonald Murders.* New York: W. W. Norton, 1995.

Prager, Linda. "Former Resident Swango Pleads Guilty to Killing Three Patients," Amednews.com. October 2, 2000.

Protzman, F. "Killing of 49 Patients by Four Nurse's Aides Stuns the Austrians." *The New York Times,* April 18, 1989.

Pyrek, Kelly. "Healthcare Serial Killers: Recognizing Red Flags," *Forensic Nurse,* September/October 2003.

Ramsland, Katherine. *The Human Predator: A Historical Chronicle of Serial Murder and Forensic Investigation.* New York: Berkley, 2005.

———. *Inside the Minds of Serial Killers: Why They Kill.* Westport, CT: Praeger, 2006.

Ramsland, Katherine and Dana DeVito. "Nurses who Kill," *Nursing Malpractice,* 3rd edition. Tucson, AZ: Lawyers & Judges Publishing, 2007, 870–893.

"Saldivar Sentenced to Six Consecutive Sentences of Life without Parole." District Attorney County of Los Angeles Media Relations News Release, March 2002.

Schechter, Harold. *Depraved: The Shocking True Story of America's First Serial Killer.* New York: Pocket, 1998.

———. *Fatal: The Poisonous Life of a Female Serial Killer.* New York: Pocket Books, 2004.

Schurman-Kauflin, Deborah. *The New Predator: Profiles of Female Serial Killers.* New York: Algora, 2000.

Scott, Gini Graham. *Homicide: One Hundred Years of Murder in America.* Los Angeles: Roxbury Park, 1998.

Stewart, James. *Blind Faith: How the Medical Establishment Let a Doctor Get away with Murder.* New York: Simon & Schuster, 1999.

Surtees, John. *The Strange Case of Dr. Bodkins Adams, and the Views of Those who Knew Him.* London: SB Publications, 2000.

"Swiss Nurse Is Sentenced for 22 Murders." *The New York Times,* January 29, 2005.

"The Death that led Shipman to the Dock." *BBC News,* January 31, 2000.

Tynan, Trudy. "Nurse's Case has Few Precedents," *Southcoast Today,* March 18, 2001.

U.S. vs. Michael J. Swango, No. 99R00496 (U.S. filed July 11, 2000).

Velinger, J. "Nurse Committed Murders to 'Test' Doctors." http://www.radio.cz/en/article/85964, May 15, 2006.

Wessinger, Catherine. *How the Millennium Comes Violently.* New York: Seven Bridges Press, 2000.

Whalen, William. *Defending Donald Harvey.* Cincinnati, OH: Emmis Books, 2005.

Whittle, Brian and Jean Ritchie, *Harold Shipman: Prescription for Murder.* London: Warner, 2000.

"Women Killed to Assure Love, One Testifies." *Detroit Free Press,* September 14, 1989.

Yorker, Beatrice C. "An Analysis of Murder Charges against Nurses." *Journal of Nursing Law* 1 (3)1994, 35–46.

———. "Nurses Accused of Murder," *American Journal of Nursing.* 1988, 1327–1332

Yorker, Beatrice C., Kenneth W. Kizer, Paula Lampe, R. Forrest, Jacquetta M. Lannan, and Donna A. Russell. "Serial Murder by Healthcare Professionals." *Journal of Forensic Science* 51 (6) 2006, 1362–1371.

Young, Filsen, ed. *The Trial of Hawley Harvey Crippen.* London: W. Hodge, 1920.

Index

About the Author

KATHERINE RAMSLAND is the author of more than 20 books including *Inside the Minds of Mass Murderers* (Praeger), *Inside the Minds of Serial Killers* (Praeger), *The Criminal Mind, The Forensic Science of CSI*, and others. She currently teaches forensic psychology at DeSales University in Pennsylvania. She is a regular feature writer for Court TV's Crime Library and has written more than three hundred articles about serial killers, forensic psychology, and forensic science.